D0553612

7.00

Leslie

1926.

*Sherwood*
*Anderson's*
# NOTEBOOK

*List of other books by*
SHERWOOD ANDERSON

---

WINDY MCPHEARSON'S SON—*A Novel* 1916
MARCHING MEN—*A Novel* 1917
MID-AMERICAN CHANTS—*Verses* 1918
WINESBURG, OHIO—*Tales* 1919
POOR WHITE—*A Novel* 1920
TRIUMPH OF THE EGG—*Tales* 1921
MANY MARRIAGES—*A Novel* 1922
HORSES AND MEN—*Tales* 1923
A STORY TELLER'S STORY—*Autobiography* 1924
DARK LAUGHTER—*A Novel* 1925

*For the Fall—1926*

"TAR"—The Story of a Mid-American Childhood. A tale of the awakening of a boy's consciousness to the world about him.

*In preparation*

ANOTHER MAN'S HOUSE—*A Novel.*

# *Sherwood Anderson's* NOTEBOOK

**Containing Articles Written During the Author's Life as a Story Teller, and Notes of his Impressions from Life & scattered through the Book**

NEW YORK MCMXXVI

BONI & LIVERIGHT

PRINTED IN THE UNITED STATES

First printing, April, 1926
Second printing, September, 1926

DEDICATED TO

TWO FRIENDS

M. D. F.

AND

JOHN EMERSON

Some of the essays, tales, fragments, notes and articles in this book have appeared in *The Literary Review*, *The Nation*, *The Survey*, *The Double Dealer*, *The New Republic*, *The Seven Arts*, *Vanity Fair*, *The Dial*. To these publications the author makes grateful acknowledgment.

## THIS BOOK CONTAINS:

*"Ahab had seventy sons in Samaria."*

*Sherwood*
*Anderson's*
# NOTEBOOK

# FOREWORD

My dear Horace Liveright,

Here is a book—my note book—I send for **FOREWORD.** you to publish in the spring if you are so minded. It is a fragmentary thing. The wind blows and water runs away under many bridges. A man should do something—in the spring.

In the meantime we scribblers occasionally become preachers. We say this or that is so and so. Sometimes some of us in America go about delivering lectures to clubs. In one place I myself spoke to a thousand people, in another place to fifteen hundred. You might have thought I was running for congress but I wasn't. What I was doing was trying to earn money to buy me a small hillside farm and plant some flowering bushes. I was salting away dollars to build a house on it too.

In some of my lectures I spoke in a most derogatory way of Mr. Henry Ford and the well-known product of his huge factory but with some of the money got so speaking I plan to buy me a Ford.

I mention this as a comfort to Mr. Ford if he has ever heard of me, which I doubt.

Well-a-day, people are so and so. They will come in large numbers to hear me talk, paying often a dollar at the gate, but when they want to read one of my books they so often borrow it from the library or from a friend.

At one place where I spoke, the chairman of the meeting highly recommended to the audience that they all borrow my books and read them.

Up I jumped shouting. "For God's sake," I cried, "if you respect me as a writer, do not borrow my books, buy them." It was ill-natured of me but there was a point I wanted to make.

The same good people would not, you see, borrow a theater ticket. They pay their fare on a railroad train. They do not go to a hotel, where they respect the cook, and ask permission to borrow a dinner.

All of this borrowing comes from the over-much making of cheap books. Can any man ever respect books again who goes in to visit a critic friend and sees the books scattered about, piled on the floor, thrown aside in heaps? I wish the critics would send them to me—freight collect. Modern books are gayly colored. They are very decorative on shelves in rooms in the country.

Go to visit in his workshop Mr. Llewellyn Jones, Mr. Stuart Sherman, Mr. Henry Mencken. (I trust Mr. Mencken and Mr. Sherman will forgive me for putting their two names thus on the same line, so warmly close to each other. I am not trying to interrupt their ancient enmity.)

To resume—my dear Horace, there they are, banked in by books.

And Mr. Robert Lovett, Mr. Glenn Frank, Mr. Rascoe, Mr. Hansen, Mr. Broun, Mr. Stallings—all buried.

There are critics I would like to see quite buried under the pile of books so that they could never crawl out but I will not mention their names. There is already too much name mentioning going on.

What I really want to say is something about this modern disregard of books.

The public is not after all to blame. If books have become a commonplace of life, like Ford cars and installment-plan furniture it comes back to the workmen in the end.

There may be extenuating circumstances for you, the publisher, and for me, the scribbler. We are caught in the hurried shoddy industrial rush like everyone else.

But we must not expect the book buyers to take our excuses into account.

The mess of cheapness into which the modern world has got is a workman's mess.

What a day it would be—the day I mean when all workmen come to a certain decision—that they would no longer put their hands to

FOREWORD. cheap materials or do cheap hurried work—for their manhood's sake.

And what a day also—when those who are so concerned with the fate of mankind quit talking so much about housing, food, starving children and wages.

As well let the body starve or freeze at once as to go on forever starving and freezing the workman impulse in men.

What I am trying to say, you see, is that the blame for the lowered taste for the book physical and for the contents of the book is too much thrown off on the public.

It is up to the workman in you the publisher and in me the writer. As you have done one book for me in such charming good taste I have no fear in thus addressing you.

The contents of the books you publish for me are up to me.

If I am not too hurried, too casual, if my own respect for my own books does not become corrupt, something of that respect is bound to carry over to the public. They will want my books to stand permanently on their shelves, will not want to borrow them.

They will be willing enough that I, the workman, get my pay as a workman, and do not have to go gabbing and gadding for my bread and cakes.

SHERWOOD ANDERSON

## FROM CHICAGO

## FROM CHICAGO [1]

*"I am mature, a man child, in America, in the west, in the great valley of the Mississippi. My head arises above the corn fields. I stand up among the new corn.*

FROM CHICAGO.

*I am a child, a confused child in a confused world. There are no clothes made that fit me. The minds of men cannot clothe me. Great projects arise within me. I have a brain and it is cunning and shrewd.*

*I want leisure to become beautiful but there is no leisure. Men should bathe me with prayers and with weeping but there are no men.*

*Now—from now—from today I shall do deeds of fiery meaning. Songs shall arise in my throat and hurt me.*

*I am a little thing, a tiny little thing on the vast prairies. I know nothing. My mouth is dirty. I cannot tell what I want. My feet are sunk in the black swampy land but I am a lover. I love life. In the end love shall save me.*

[1] Written in 1916. Published in *Seven Arts Magazine.*

*The days are long. It rains. It snows. I am an old man. I am sweeping the ground where my grave shall be.*

*Look upon me, my beloved, my lover who does not come. I am raw and bleeding, a new thing in a new world. I run swiftly over bare fields. Listen! There is the sound of the tramping of many feet. Life is dying in me. I am old and palsied. I am just at the beginning of my life.*

*Do you not see that I am old, oh my beloved? Do you not understand that I cannot sing, that my songs choke me? Do you not see that I am so young I cannot find the word in the confusion of words?"*

MID-AMERICAN CHANTS.

## 1

WHILE he is still young and pregnant with life it behooves a man to attempt to extend the province of his life through his work; and the attempt may fairly be said to fall under the head of an effort to extend the possibilities of all life.

What to the living is more sweetly vital than life? Fearing as all true men do and must the danger of the approach of that self-satisfaction that is death, the young man will find upon this road difficulties that destroy self-satisfaction. Knowing that all about him in the world are men and women striving to fasten upon him their own insanity of conformity, the young and valiant soul will find here a constant demand upon his resources that will be to him a tonic against the insidious poison of association with the weak.

The driving impulse is, I should say, something like this—that a man, having taught himself to look keenly and constantly at himself, must realize that of all the figures in the world his is the most fortunate. Standing upon the high place and watching the struggle of his soul upon the wall of life, the young man, among all men so standing, knows that his soul has at least the chance of success in the struggle.

In a quite practical way also the young man whose imagination is still alive is one upon whom riches have been bestowed. Does he arise in the morning half ill of the perplexities of his life, a half hour of surrender to the impulses always being awakened within by the play of his imagination shall restore him. By a bridge near a river he stands and is stirred by the sight of the giant mechanism by which the bridge is raised for the passage of a ship. His quick imagination sees the workers in the great factories making the mechanism. If by good fortune he has been at some time also a laborer he hears in fancy the crashing blows of the great hammers and sees the beauty of the bodies of men absorbed in physical tasks. What to him at the moment is the fact that the laborer is cheated of the reward of his labor or that his own coat is somewhat shabby? In a flash his fancy has restored to him the sweetness of a day. One of a million little beauties of every street scene or of every country roadside has revealed itself to him.

By his side stand men who are waiting for the footway over the bridge to be reëstablished that they may cross the river. One of them, a plumber, has a heavy wrench in his hand. He begins talking to a second man and speaking of the ship that is passing. He uses nautical terms, throwing them about with more zeal than skill. The imaginative man turns quickly. A light dances in his eyes. He has seen behind the plumber, who is young and muscular, a pretty waitress. He knows that the young male is but swaggering before the female, that he is not trying to deceive the men in the crowd by his assumed knowledge of ships but is honestly striving to awaken admiration in the mind of the woman. One of the hundred little interplays of human relations with which each of the imaginative man's living hours is colored has come to take his mind off the rather second-rate breakfast he must eat.

In all of the concerns of his life, in the perplexities of love, in the muddle of affairs that compel him to spend hours, to him divinely precious, in the treadmill of making a living, the living fancy of the young dreamer is as a strong arm protecting him.

And so the young man having within him youth and the courage that has made him a dreamer, begins to aspire, humbly and for the most part in secret, to make to life some return for the riches that have been given him. If he be a craftsman he will be at first appalled by the difficulties of the task to which he sets himself. Old masters, men long dead, strong true men have put in his hand a tool so fitting to the work he wants to do that it seems at times absurd that he should strive to make for himself his own tools. The names of old workmen dance before him. To attempt where they have accomplished seems a kind of sacrilege. If he be of a fine quality and set upon modesty the young man will make the attempt but will make it with a certain humbleness and always, first of all, for the fun of making it.

## 2

The novelist is about to begin the writing of a novel. For a year he will be at the task and what a year he will have. He is going to write the story of Virginia Borden, daughter of Fan Borden, a Missouri river raftsman. There in his little room he sits, a small hunched up figure with a pencil in his hand. He has never learned to run a typewriter and so he will write the words slowly and painfully, one after another, on the white paper.

What a multitude of words! For hours he will sit perfectly still, writing madly and throwing the sheets about. That is the happy time. The madness has possession of him. People will come in at the door and sit about, talking and laughing. Sometimes he jumps out of his chair and walks up and down. He lights and relights his pipe. Overcome with weariness he goes forth to walk. When he walks he carries a heavy black walking-stick and goes muttering along.

The novelist tries to shake off his madness but he does not succeed. In a store he buys more writing paper and, sitting on a stone near where some men are building a house, begins again to write. He talks aloud and occasionally fingers a lock of hair that falls down over his eyes. He lets his pipe go out and relights it nervously.

Days pass. It is raining and again the novelist is in his room writing. After a long evening of work he throws all he has written away.

What is the secret of the madness of the writer?

He is a small man and has a torn ear. A part of his ear has been carried away by the explosion of a gun. Above the ear there is a spot, as large as a child's hand, where no hair grows.

The novelist is a clerk in a store in Wabash Avenue in Chicago. When he was quite young he began to clerk in the store and for a time promised to be successful. He sold goods and there was something in his smile that won its way into hearts. He was interested in the people who came into the store and the people liked him for his interest.

In the store now the novelist does not promise success. There is a kind of conspiracy. Although he tries earnestly he makes mistakes, and all of his fellows conspire to forgive and conceal his mistakes. Sometimes when he has muddled things badly they are impatient and the manager of the store, a huge fat fellow with thin gray hair, takes him into a room and scolds him.

The two men sit by a window and look down into Wabash Avenue. It is snowing and people hurry along with bowed heads. So much do the novelist and the fat gray-haired man like each other that the scolding does not last. They begin to talk and the hours pass. Presently it is time to close the store for the night and the two go down a flight of stairs to the street.

FROM CHICAGO.

On a corner stand the novelist and the storekeeper, still talking, and presently they go together to dine. The manager of the store looks at his watch and it is eight o'clock. He remembers a dinner engagement made with his wife and hurries away. On the street car he blames himself for his carelessness. "I should not have tried to reprimand the fellow," he says, and laughs.

It is night and the novelist works in his room. The night is cold but he opens his window. There is, in his closet, a torn woollen jacket given him by a friend and he wraps the jacket about him. It has stopped snowing and the stars are in the sky.

The talk with the store manager has inflamed his mind. Again he writes furiously. What he is now writing will not fit into the life-story of Virginia Borden, but, for the moment, he thinks it will and he is happy. Tomorrow he will throw all away but that will not destroy his dream.

Who is this Virginia Borden of whom the novelist writes and why does he write of her? He does not know that he will get money for his story and he is growing old. What a foolish affair. Presently there may be a new manager in the store and the novelist will lose his place. Once in a long while he thinks of that and shivers with cold.

The novelist is not to be won from his purpose. Virginia Borden is a woman who lived in Chicago. The novelist has seen and talked with her. Like the store manager she forgot herself talking to him. She forgot the torn ear and the bare spot where no hair grew and the skin was snow-white. To talk with the novelist was like talking aloud to herself. It was delightful. For a year she knew him and then went away to live with a brother in Colorado where she was thrown from a horse and killed.

When she lived in Chicago many people knew Virginia Borden. They saw her going here and there in the streets. Once she was married to a man who was leader of an orchestra in a theater but the marriage was not a success. Nothing that Virginia Borden did in the city was successful.

The novelist is to write the life-story of Virginia Borden. As he begins the task a great humbleness creeps over him. He is afraid and trembles.

In the woman who walked and talked with him the novelist has seen many strange, beautiful, unexpected little turns of the mind and the body. He knows that in Virginia Borden there was a spirit that, but for the muddle of life, might have become a flame. To him her body was a flame at which he warmed himself when he was cold.

It is the dream of the novelist that he will

FROM CHICAGO. make men understand his feeling for the woman they saw in the streets. He wants to tell the store manager of her and the little wiry man who has a desk next his own. In the Wabash Avenue store there is a woman who sits on a high stool with her back to the novelist. He wants to tell her of Virginia Borden, to make her feel the reality of his own sense of the woman's beauty, to make all see that such a woman once lived and went about among the women of Chicago.

As the novelist works events grow in his mind. His mind is forever active and he is continually making up stories about himself. As the Virginia Borden men saw was but a caricature of the Virginia Borden who lived in the mind of the novelist, so he knows that he is himself but a shadow of something very real.

And so the novelist puts himself into the book. In the book he is a large, square-shouldered man with tiny eyes. He is one who came to Chicago from a village in Poland and was a leader in an orchestra in the theater. As the orchestra leader, the novelist married Virginia Borden and lived in a house with her.

You see the novelist wants to explain himself also. He is a lover and so vividly does he love that he has the courage to love even himself. And so it is the lover who sits writing and the madness of the writer is the madness of the lover. As he writes he is making love. Surely all can understand that.

3

Consider the tantalizing difference in the quality of work produced by two men. In the first we get at times an almost overwhelming sense of proficiency in his craft. The writer, we feel, knows form, knows construction, knows words. How he slings the words about. Almost every one of his lines is quotable.

And this other fellow. His words do not cling, his art forms become at times shapeless, he stumbles, going crudely and awkwardly forward.

And how breathlessly we follow. What is he doing that he holds us so tightly? What is the secret of our love of him, even in the midst of his awkwardness?

He is revealing himself to us. See how shamelessly and boldly he is trying to tell us of the thing that is a never-ceasing marvel to him—the march of his own life, the complete story of his own adventure in the midst of the universal adventure.

4

It is Sunday evening and I am dining alone in a restaurant. The day is cold and cheerless

FROM CHICAGO.

and since morning I have been at work in my room.

I have been revising a book that is partly good, partly bad. That it is at all bad has chilled the fires in me. The thing should not have been bad. What a fine figure I was as the labor leader. How strange and wonderful my thoughts as I went through the city nights, hurrying from place to place, stirring the soul of labor. And how feebly I have expressed my thoughts. In the restaurant I jab at the tablecloth with my fork. "I should have done more with myself in so fine a rôle."

Some two weeks before that evening I had met a woman in another restaurant. She was an Englishwoman with a long thin face and when I came upon her she sat at a table with a party of friends. One of the party beckoned and I went to sit at the table. I sat by the Englishwoman.

Between the Englishwoman and myself much laughing talk. Here and there we turned, laughing and shouting at the people seated at the table.

And then in a moment all was changed. A new quality came to color our brief acquaintanceship. There amid the noise and the laughter our two bodies ran out to meet each other. For five, perhaps for ten minutes we sat stupidly looking at each other. Like two

FROM CHICAGO.

wide-eyed children in a world full of unaccountable people and impulses we tried to be intellectual. We talked, I have forgotten of what, and all the time something inside us kept meeting and embracing.

"We must talk a whole evening away," I pleaded, thinking still it was talk we both wanted. "After these few moments we would be fools not to do that."

The hand of the woman, lying on the table, trembled. My hand trembled also. Even now as I sit writing of the woman, my hand, that plays back and forth on the paper, shakes with the memory of her.

We walked in Jackson Park in Chicago, going along the paths in silence. How dark it was. In so brief a time there had been built up in each of us a background of much feeling. Already our two lives were colored, each by the other. After a time words came. She was lonely in America and talked of her own country and of a wide moor that ran away toward the sunset beyond her own town. On Sundays she had gone upon the moor with the people with whom she lived and whom she loved. With a man she loved she had walked hand in hand and had talked as she and I had talked in the restaurant.

In the park it was cold and dark and we met no people. Presently we got upon a wide open space. The dreary persistent wind roared in distant trees. In the night the open space was mysteriously vast.

Again we walked along in silence. I put out my hand and in it she put her hand.

And then another problem presented itself to the woman and me. We had stopped beneath a small tree. Away in the distance a street car ran past the front of the park. It seemed immeasurable miles away. The cold wind beat about her slender figure.

I took the woman into my arms. In her face as it looked up into mine was all of the loveliness of woman. How I longed for beauty within myself, beauty with which to match her beauty, the quiet, submissive, waiting loveliness in her.

When it passed I took her by the hand and led her back to walk again upon gravel paths.

We talked then. Words welled up in me. "Never," I cried, "shall I find beauty to match your beauty." Aimlessly I stumbled about, saying words, trying to make her understand how truly in my poor way I loved her.

In the restaurant I pay my bill, and go out into the street. What matter if my hands tremble and I have forgotten to eat? What matter if the woman of the park later got lost in the rush of Chicago? What matter if I never saw such a woman, if I merely walked alone in the windswept park? What matter if I never in all my life knew such a woman?

Is my story for all these reasons the less true? Is the moment in which I look down into the loveliness of a woman's eyes less a part of my life because it happened in fancy?

5

I am walking in the street at evening of a summer day. The rush of people homeward bound has passed and something of the jaded weariness of their faces remains in my mind. I go heavily along by an iron railing that guards a network of railroad tracks. The tracks run away between rows of gray brick buildings into Chicago's West Side. Beside the tracks is the river that flows from the lake into the land and that carries away the sewage of the city. The river is like a drain that takes the fetid matter from a wound and the city is a wound upon the prairie.

As I walk my mind becomes heavy and dull. I have passed the middle age of life and I begin to measure the courage left to me as a traveler in a desert might look at the water in a water-bottle. I become afraid and tremble. Over a distant bridge that mounts high above the river and the tracks passes a long procession of

FROM CHICAGO. trucks. From the wheels of wagons dust arises. Behind the cloud of dust burns the sun, also flushed with weariness.

In a kind of desperation I begin letting my mind play with my own life, with what I have seen of the lives of others. Things seen and that have been lying like spermatozoa in the sac of my mind grow and are fertilized by the facts of my own journey through the world.

I am a boy who came to Chicago from a little place in Missouri. Like most boys raised in the hill country I was lean and strong. I was uneducated but much solitary riding of horses over lonely hills had let me into the habit of letting my mind play. It was a custom of mine to talk aloud and to sing at the top of my voice as I went along and at times it was difficult to restrain these impulses as I walked among the crowds in the city streets.

In the city I lived on the West Side with my sister who later went wrong and was lost in the maze of the life there. Our younger sister, who is now married to a printer and lives in a suburb called Austin, lived with us. She had blue eyes and a tiny hesitating voice and on Sunday mornings walked hand in hand with me in Washington Boulevard, chattering away and asking questions that I could not answer.

What a struggle we had, the three of us, in

the city. For a long time I could not get work and we got into debt so that I had to write to my uncle for money. He sold three hogs that would have littered in the spring and sent the money to me. Sometimes I smile now as I think of that letter. How the words must have been misspelled and how amusing the arrangement of the words. It might have been printed in a comic paper. Later, you see, I went to night school and rose in the world.

FROM CHICAGO.

But I am thinking of that first winter. I worked with other men on a pile-driver that drove piles for the foundation of a warehouse. The warehouse is now finished and stands near the mouth of the river where the boats come in from the lake. All day the waves washed against the long flat boat on which stood the engine that lifted a heavy weight only to let it drop again on the head of the log we were driving into the soft river mud. At first the log sank rapidly, a foot or more with each blow, but later it went slowly, inch by inch.

How cold it was on the boat. In the morning I liked it out there. The slapping of the waves against the boat, the heavy thump of the weight on the head of the log and the puffing of the engine made it possible to talk aloud.

I talked out everything that came into my mind. Close behind the engine I stood and the

FROM CHICAGO. words rolled out of me. In the midst of the many noises there was a great silence, so I talked into that, telling of my hopes, my dreams, my strangely impossible ambitions in life.

There was a woman of thirty-five who sang in the choir in a church on our street and I talked of her. When she sang on Sunday mornings she sometimes put her hand on the little railing of the choir loft and from the seat where I sat with my younger blue-eyed sister I could see her fingers peeping out. When I talked of her hands, out there in the noisy place on the boat, I sometimes took off my gloves and looked at my own hands. They were strong but the skin was very coarse and in places the skin was broken so that red angry flesh looked through. The skin at the edge of the wounds was like the white of the belly of a fish. The water did that.

I am thinking of the winter nights when I came away from the boat, going to my place on the West Side. I went along the railroad tracks just below where I am standing now. It was dark and only the lights at the switches, the red and green railroad lights, lighted the way.

On the boat at the edge of the lake I did not talk and sing after three o'clock in the afternoon. Those were the bad hours, from three until six, when we quit and went along boards to a wharf. From the wharf we stumbled up to a spur of railroad tracks. Once I fell off the boards and had to be fished out of the water but even that did not increase my numbness.

All day the waves that beat against the boat sent a fine spray of water over us and this froze into ice. When the wind was off shore, however, it was not so bad. In the morning the heart beat stoutly, but after three o'clock the feet and the hands and even the balls of the eyes became cold. I could not think of the woman who sang in the church choir after three o'clock and sometimes as I went along the tracks that ran into the West Side I could not see very well. How odd that a train did not hit me! I stepped away from trains like a horse that cannot be induced to run its head against a tree, even in the black darkness.

From the place by the railing at the edge of the tracks on the summer evening I return across the city to my own room. I am vividly aware of my own life that escaped the winter on the boat. How many such lives I have lived. Then I only made a dollar and a half a day and now I sometimes make more than that in a few minutes. How wonderful to be able to write words. I am enamored of myself because I can write words and can make my living by it. Now perhaps I could have the woman who sang in the choir and perhaps I would not take her if she offered.

6

In my room I sit thinking of courage—of the courage of men. The balls of the eyes of the boy on the track were numb and he could scarcely see. In the two rooms where he lived with his sisters there was a tiny coal stove by a window. It was put there to stop the cold from coming through the cracks in the window sill and that necessitated a long stovepipe having many joints. The pipe was fastened with wires and often at night it fell down scattering black coal soot on the bed where the boy lay. He could not eat when he came home but lay on the bed until his heart beat strong again and warmth came back into his body. At nine o'clock he arose, washed, had his supper, and returned again to sleep beneath the long stove-pipe.

7

On my desk in my room there is a black leather note-book with leaves that may be taken out. When the leaves are all written full I take them out, fasten them with rubber bands, and put them away. Then I fill the book with new white leaves.

In my room when I come back from standing

FROM CHICAGO.

by the tracks I think how I was afraid because I had reached middle age. There is a cunning satisfaction in my heart because I think that when my body is weary I shall take the leaves from the rubber bands and go on publishing year after year as though I were yet alive.

There is satisfaction in this thought until another thought comes. Not as I stood weary by the tracks, but now, as I think of the hoarded leaves of white paper in the rubber bands, has the coward appeared. To myself I say, "Am I to be less stout-hearted than the boy who stumbled half frozen along the tracks?"

Are we, who write stories, who paint pictures and who act upon the stage to go on forever hoarding our minor triumphs like frugal merchants who keep a secret bank account, are we to be less courageous than our brothers, the laborers?

## 8

It is three o'clock of a winter's afternoon and I am lying in a nook among rocks on the side of a mountain in Missouri. I am wearing heavy boots that lace to the knees and they are covered with frozen mud. In a road far below an old Ozark mountaineer is riding a mule to a distant town. He is a tall old man and his feet hang to the ground. I am in a sheltered place and

FROM CHICAGO. the cold wind does not reach me, but across the prospect of barren hills it goes, shouting and roaring. Beyond the road that lies at the foot of the hill there is a river and along this comes presently a raft upon which stands a man with a pole in his hand. He is singing a ballad of a country girl who went away to a distant city and there became the plaything of lust. There is a penetrating quality of beauty in the raftsman's voice and my mind is carried away by it.

I begin reconstructing the life of the country girl of the song. She is tall and strong and very lean, like the girls I have seen at the doors of the cabins along the roads that run through the hills. There is in her a kind of wild beauty, tempered by ignorance and coarseness. She stands within the door of the cabin, also singing, and outside the door, clad in a worn man's overcoat, is an old woman who smokes a pipe. As she sings the mountain girl looks at the old woman, who is hideous. The hunger for beauty, that will presently destroy the girl, that echoes in the heart of the lonely raftsman on the river among the hills, comes up and possesses me. I turn about in my nook and stare long and hard at the cheerless hills. The oak trees have retained last year's leaves and these are now a dull red. I see death here as I have seen it so often in faces of men in the cities, but here the note of

beauty has remained in the midst of death. The 
dull red leaves that rattle in the wind are the visible signs of it. It plays in the minds of the raftsman and the girl, and in my own mind.

Again I begin the endless game of reconstructing my own life, jerking it out of the shell that dies, striving to breathe into it beauty and meaning. A thought comes to me.

When I was a boy I lived in a town in Ohio and often I wandered away to lie upon my back, thinking, as I am doing now. I reconstruct and begin to color and illuminate incidents of my life there. Words said, shouts of children, the barking of dogs at night, occasional flashes of beauty in the eyes of women and old men are remembered. I wonder why my life, why all lives, are not more beautiful.

Away to the city I take myself and I am sitting beside a woman in a room upstairs in a cheap apartment house. I am a grown man now, alive with vigor, and I am determined I shall possess the woman. She has a tall boyish figure and strange gray eyes. Something in the eyes maddens me. I rush to the woman, take her into my arms, and kiss her passionately. I have succeeded in my purpose, have killed something that was lovely in the eyes of the woman. Although she dressed as a woman she was not wholly a woman and did not want what

I wanted. I have forced her. I have done my share toward putting that keen plaintive note into the voice of the ignorant raftsman. I am always doing that; like others I shall always be doing it, but was it not the plaintive note that made the beauty of the song?

# FOUR AMERICAN IMPRESSIONS

# FOUR AMERICAN IMPRESSIONS[1]

## GERTRUDE STEIN, PAUL ROSENFELD, RING LARDNER, SINCLAIR LEWIS

### 1

FOUR AMERICAN IMPRESSIONS.

ONE who thinks a great deal about people and what they are up to in the world comes inevitably in time to relate them to experiences connected with his own life. The round hard apples in this old orchard are the breasts of my beloved. The curved round hill in the distance is the body of my beloved, lying asleep. I cannot avoid practicing this trick of lifting people out of the spots on which in actual life they stand and transferring them to what seems at the moment some more fitting spot in the fanciful world.

And I get also a kind of aroma from people. They are green healthy growing things or they have begun to decay. There is something in this man, to whom I have just talked, that has sent me away from him smiling and in an odd way pleased with myself. Why has this other man,

[1] Written in 1919. Published in *The New Republic.*

although his words were kindly and his deeds apparently good, spread a cloud over my sky?

In my own boyhood in an Ohio town I went about delivering newspapers at kitchen doors, and there were certain houses to which I went—old brick houses with immense old-fashioned kitchens—in which I loved to linger. On Saturday mornings I sometimes managed to collect a fragrant cooky at such a place but there was something else that held me. Something got into my mind connected with the great light kitchens and the women working in them that came sharply back when, last year, I went to visit an American woman, Miss Gertrude Stein, in her own large room in the house at 27 rue de Fleurus in Paris. In the great kitchen of my fanciful world in which, ever since that morning, I have seen Miss Stein standing there is a most sweet and gracious aroma. Along the walls are many shining pots and pans, and there are innumerable jars of fruits, jellies and preserves. Something is going on in the great room, for Miss Stein is a worker in words with the same loving touch in her strong fingers that was characteristic of the women of the kitchens of the brick houses in the town of my boyhood. She is an American woman of the old sort, one who cares for the handmade goodies and who scorns the factory-made foods, and in her own great kitchen she is making something with her materials, something sweet to the tongue and fragrant to the nostrils.

That her materials are the words of our English speech and that we do not, most of us, know or care too much what she is up to does not greatly matter to me. The impression I wish now to give you of her is of one very intent and earnest in a matter most of us have forgotten. She is laying word against word, relating sound to sound, feeling for the taste, the smell, the rhythm of the individual word. She is attempting to do something for the writers of our English speech that may be better understood after a time, and she is not in a hurry.

And I have always that picture of the woman in the great kitchen of words, standing there by a table, clean, strong, with red cheeks and sturdy legs, always quietly and smilingly at work. If her smile has in it something of the mystery, to the male a least, of the Mona Lisa, I remember that the women in the kitchens on the wintry mornings wore often that same smile.

She is making new, strange and to my ears sweet combinations of words. As an American writer I admire her because she, in her person, represents something sweet and healthy in our American life, and because I have a kind of undying faith that what she is up to in her word kitchen in Paris is of more importance to writers of English than the work of many of our more easily understood and more widely accepted word artists.

## 2

When it comes to our Mr. Ring Lardner, here is something else again. Here is another word fellow, one who cares about the words of our American speech and who is perhaps doing more than any other American to give new force to the words of our everyday life.

There is something I think I understand about Mr. Ring Lardner. The truth is that I believe there is something the matter with him and I have a fancy I know what it is. He is afraid of the highbrows. They scare him to death. I wonder why. For it is true that there is often, in a paragraph of his, more understanding of life, more human sympathy, more salty wisdom than in hundreds of pages of, say Mr. Sinclair Lewis's dreary prose—and I am sure Mr. Lewis would not hesitate to outface any highbrow in his lair.

I said that I thought I knew what was the matter with Mr. Ring Lardner. He comes from out in my country, from just such another town as the one in which I spent my own boyhood, and I remember certain shy lads of my own town who always made it a point to consort mostly with the town toughs—and for a reason. There was in them something extremely sensitive that did not want to be hurt. Even to mention the fact that there was in such a one a real love of life, a quick sharp stinging hunger for beauty would have sent a blush of shame to his cheeks. He was intent upon covering up, concealing from everyone, at any cost, the shy hungry child he was carrying about within himself.

And I always see our Mr. Ring Lardner as such a fellow. He is covering up, sticking to the gang, keeping out of sight. And that is all right too, if in secret and in his suburban home he is really using his talent for sympathetic understanding of life, if in secret he is being another Mark Twain and working in secret on his own *Huckleberry Finn.* Mark Twain wrote and was proclaimed for writing his *Innocents Abroad, Following the Equator, Roughing It,* etc., etc., and was during his lifetime most widely recognized for such secondary work. And Mark Twain was just such another shy lad, bluffed by the highbrows—and even the glorious Mark had no more sensitive understanding of the fellow in the street, in the hooch joint, the ballpark and the city suburb than our Mr. Ring Lardner.

## 3

FOUR AMERICAN IMPRESSIONS.

Which brings me to a man who, it seems to me, of all our American writers, is the one who is most unafraid, Mr. Paul Rosenfeld. Here is an American writer actually unashamed of being fine and sensitive in his work. To me it seems that he has really freed himself from both the high and the low brows and has made of himself a real aristocrat among writers of prose.

To be sure, to the man in the street, accustomed to the sloppiness of hurried newspaper writing, the Rosenfeld prose is sometimes difficult. His vocabulary is immense and he cares very, very much for just the shade of meaning he is striving to convey. Miss Jean Heap recently spoke of him as "our well dressed writer of prose," and I should think Paul Rosenfeld would not too much resent the connotations of that. For, after all, Rosenfeld is our man of distinction, the American, it seems to me, who is unafraid and unashamed to live for the things of the spirit as expressed in the arts. I get him as the man walking cleanly and boldly and really accepting, daring to accept, the obligations of the civilized man. To my ears that acceptance has made his prose sound clearly and sweetly across many barren fields. To me it is often like soft bells heard ringing at evening across fields long let go to the weeds of carelessness and the general slam-it-throughness of so much of our American writing.

4

Of the four American writers concerning whose handling of our speech I have had the temerity to express my own feeling there is left Mr. Sinclair Lewis.

The texture of the prose written by Mr. Lewis gives me but faint joy and I cannot escape the conviction that for some reason Lewis has himself found but little joy, either in life among us or in his own effort to channel his reactions to our life into prose. There can be no doubt that this man, with his sharp journalistic nose for news of the outer surface of our lives, has found out a lot of things about us and the way we live in our towns and cities, but I am very sure that in the life of every man woman and child in the country there are forces at work that seem to have escaped the notice of Mr. Lewis. Mr. Ring Lardner has seen them and in his writing there is sometimes real laughter, but one has the feeling that Lewis never laughs at all, that he is in an odd way too serious about something to laugh.

For after all, even in Gopher Prairie or in Indianapolis, Indiana, boys go swimming in the creeks on summer afternoons, shadows play at evening on factory walls, old men dig angleworms and go fishing together, love comes to at least a few men and women, and everything else failing, the baseball club comes from a neighboring town and Tom Robinson gets a home run. That's something. There is an outlook on life across which even the cry of a child, choked to death by its own mother, would be something. Life in our American towns and cities is barren enough and there are enough people saying that with the growth of industrialism it has become continually more and more ugly, but Mr. Paul Rosenfeld and Mr. Ring Lardner apparently do not find it altogether barren and ugly. For them and for a growing number of men and women in America there is something like a dawn that Mr. Lewis has apparently sensed but little, for there is so little sense of it in the texture of his prose. Reading Mr. Sinclair Lewis, one comes inevitably to the conclusion that here is a man writing who, wanting passionately to love the life about him, cannot bring himself to do so, and who, wanting perhaps to see beauty descend upon our lives like a rainstorm, has become blind to the minor beauties our lives hold.

And is it not just this sense of dreary spiritual death in the man's work that is making it so widely read? To one who is himself afraid to live there is, I am sure, a kind of joy in

seeing other men as dead. In my own feeling for the man from whose pen has come all of this prose over which there are so few lights and shades, I have come at last to sense, most of all, the man fighting terrifically and ineffectually for a thing about which he really does care. There is a kind of fighter living inside Mr. Sinclair Lewis and there is, even in this dull, unlighted prose of his, a kind of dawn coming. In the dreary ocean of this prose, islands begin to appear. In *Babbitt* there are moments when the people of whom he writes, with such amazing attention to the outer details of lives, begin to think and feel a little, and with the coming of life into his people a kind of nervous, hurried beauty and life flits, like a lantern carried by a night watchman past the window of a factory as one stands waiting and watching in a grim street on a night of December.

NOTES OUT OF A MAN'S LIFE

# NOTES OUT OF A MAN'S LIFE [1]

## NOTE 1

THIS book has become my confessional. Formerly I tried in another book—unpublished—to make what I called a Testament.

NOTES OUT OF A MAN'S LIFE.

I tried to do it in song but the song broke.

The making of a testament, or rather a confession, is a kind of relief.

When I go into a church I find myself unable to kneel before a priest or a preacher. As the need of a symbol has been strong in me I have tried other things. I have been in turn a river worshiper, a moon and sun worshiper, a mountain worshiper. Often I have followed a child through the streets.

Once when I had been drunk and had been with a so-called fallen woman I did something that nearly led to my arrest.

Nearly all physically strong men have periods of pure flesh worship. I had been in such a period and had picked up a woman in the streets.

[1] New Orleans. Spring, 1924.

She did not understand my mood. Why should she understand? This was in Chicago. We went into a house and I stayed there all night. I tried to talk with her, to tell her something of my young man's impulses, of the confusion in me that had led me to her but she could not understand. She had been cheated, buffeted, beaten.

All prostitutes are morons. The clever, alive prostitute of fiction does not exist in fact. Writers are prone to be sentimental about prostitution because they spend so much of their own lives walking close to the line of their own kind of prostitution.

When I had been with the woman all night I left in the early morning. The sun was shining brightly. In the streets children were playing.

That day I got drunk and in the afternoon went into a park. Seeing a child with its mother I followed.

At last I ran to the child and falling on my knees tried to apologize.

It was not understood. People thought me insane. Kneeling before the child I muttered a few words about life, the sources of life and how they were befouled.

The mother, being frightened, screamed—the child stared at me.

I escaped through bushes and running a long way got into a street car.

. . . . . .

I had to laugh at myself and you will laugh.

It doesn't bother me—not now.

At last after seeking many confessionals I came to paper. I am humble before these sheets. They are clean.

I write my testament upon them. It is all I can do.

## NOTE 2

Many men I know who are without leisure constantly cry out for it, not knowing the responsibilities of leisure. Responsibilities to whom? To oneself, alas.

How many men have told me they wanted leisure to write poetry.

Great God!

The amount of physical labor needed to make a man widely known as a poet of merit is infinitesimal. All the actual physical labor of writing done by the greatest and most profound of poets could be done by any average newspaper man during any average month of work.

Leisure achieved ends in what? "I have this time on my hands now. What shall I do with it?"

"I shall walk about, seeing men at work, talking to men."

"But why am I not at work?"

To the man of sensibilities there is too much time left to think of self.

I myself go about playing at life. I am a young boy, a vagrant picked up by the police.

I am in a cell with drunken negro women, with white women, prostitutes, thieves.

Now I am standing before a judge. "What excuse have you for being alive, for cluttering the streets?"

"But occasionally I tell tales, have them printed in books."

"What of that? Does not every one tell tales? Is it an excuse for not being at work?"

"Men live by carving wood, pounding iron, steering ships, plowing the ground, building houses. When they are not so employed they sometimes sing, tell tales."

"But I am a judge and it is my business to pass judgment. I pronounce you a guilty man."

"Oh judge, you are quite right. I am a vagrant, a no-account.

"But you see, judge, there are no houses being built. Men do not carve wood, shape iron, steer ships. All that is at an end. It is done by radio now."

The judge is as puzzled by life as I am. He

also is a vagrant. Something has got out of the hands of men.

For ages now men have cried out for leisure. One of these days the impatient gods will punish men by giving it to them.

## NOTE 3

A book or story, when you are writing it, must get to the place where reading what you have already written excites you to write more.

If you come to a day when you cannot write, do not try. If you force yourself what you write at such times will poison all the future pages. If you do write at such times throw all away.

Every writer should say to himself every morning, "I do not have to write. I can be a tramp."

When a story gets to the place where reading over what you have written excites you to write more it has done what I call "come alive."

It will go now if you let it. Be patient. Go talk to men. Go fishing or swimming. When your fingers itch run home to your desk and write again.

I write down rules like this because I break them so often and when I do break them I feel such a fool.

## NOTE 4

NOTES OUT OF A MAN'S LIFE.

When I am not writing all my instincts lead me to go where men are working with their hands. Formerly I also worked with my hands, touched to some purpose wood, iron, brass, brick, stone, the earth. That one should get money by writing, painting, making music is in some way false.

I love rich delicate fabrics and carpets, love to touch such things with my fingers but why should I possess them?

As an outcast in the world of men, working my way from place to place, I was uncomfortable but happy.

In the south, where I now live, it seems to me the negroes, who do all the hard work, are the sweetest people.

I cannot approach the negro, cannot speak intimately with him. Such an attempt on my part would arouse the suspicions of both whites and blacks.

I stand aside, make myself as much as I can a part of the wharves, the streets, the fields where these men and women work.

Others feel as I feel. A southern woman writer, of what is called a distinguished family down here, whispered to me across a dinner table. "What, if you were not yourself, would you like to be?" I had asked her, making conversation.

"Above all things I should like to be a negro woman," she said.

I talked to a southern man, the son of a planter. For a long time he had been at work on a novel. It was smart and clever. That was not what he wanted it to be. "If there is ever an art produced in the American south it must come from the negro," he said.

I dress in as fine linen as I can afford, wear bright ties, loud socks, carry a cane. The negroes on the docks among whom I spend so much of my time like me so. I can see the looks of approval pass from eye to eye. We have something in common. Together we love bright gaudy colors, food, the earth, the sky, the river. We love song and laughter, night, drink, and lust.

## NOTE 5

It is hopeless for me to dream of becoming an aristocrat. When I have much money in my pockets I feel like apologizing to every man and woman I meet. The wealthy never make me really envious.

I remember a time spent in the home of a rich man. That was just after I had done what is called "raising myself from the ranks of labor."

I had been reading George Moore, Oscar Wilde, Henry James,—had decided I would devote myself to becoming delicate-minded, an aristocrat.

I was in the house of the rich man and it was evening. I remember his wife's dress, how lovely it was. I kept wanting to touch it. She had full lips, eyes like half faded flowers seen along paths in the forest on hot summer days and long slender fingers on which were finely wrought rings.

We talked of books. The woman had a kind of admiration for me because I had written books that had been published. How foolish of her. Her husband had shrewd hard eyes and was a collector of first editions.

After we had dined several people came in and there was more talk. I talked foolishly, trying to appear clever. At last the evening passed and I was shown to a room. I had never slept in such a room before. Sleep would not come.

I thought of the woman's eyes, of her husband's eyes. After sitting for a long time by a window I got up and ran about the room touching everything with my fingers.

I touched the bed hangings, the chairs, the carpet, the window curtains. Many single things in the room had cost more money than I had been able to earn by years of labor with my hands.

That did not matter. I did not feel at home, did not feel comfortable. When all the house was asleep I tiptoed into a hallway. A servant caught me creeping along the hallway. I stammered some poor excuse, that I wanted to go into the grounds for a walk.

Outside the grounds were lovely but there was a high iron fence and I was still uncomfortable. I climbed the fence and just as I reached the top looked back toward the house. Through a window I saw the woman standing in her night dress in a room. She was weeping. It was an unhappy household. Had that driven me away?

Leaping down from the fence I walked for a long way in a dusty road. I had left my bag with my few belongings. Beside the road was a railroad and in a creek some men were fishing. They had set out night lines and had built a fire. They were drinking and as I passed broke out into a song. It was one o'clock.

That is all. Nothing else happened. I got on a train and went to another town where I slept in a workingman's hotel. The furniture was ugly and I did not like that but I had got back among people to whom I belonged.

I belong to men who work with their hands, to negroes, to poor women—the wives of workers, heavy with child, with work-weary faces. Often I think them more lovely than any aristocrat, any man or woman of leisure I have ever seen. That they do not understand what I feel and do not know their own beauty when it flashes forth does not matter. I belong to them whether they will have me or not.

As to the rich man and his wife, I met them once in another house and they acted strangely. The man was angry and the woman embarrassed. She had still her own kind of impersonal beauty but it did not touch me. We were left alone together for a moment and she wanted to speak of what happened. "You know how to be cruel, how to punish people," she said suddenly, but I thought she had missed the point and I did not answer.

# A NOTE ON REALISM

# A NOTE ON REALISM[1]



THERE is something very confusing to both readers and writers about the notion of realism in fiction. As generally understood it is akin to what is called "representation" in painting. The fact is before you and you put it down, adding a high spot here and there, to be sure. No man can quite make himself a camera. Even the most realistic worker pays some tribute to what is called "art." Where does representation end and art begin? The location of the line is often as confusing to practicing artists as it is to the public.

Recently a young writer came to talk with me about our mutual craft. He spoke with enthusiastic admiration of a certain book—very popular a year or two ago. "It is the very life. So closely observed. It is the sort of thing I should like to do. I should like to bring life itself within the pages of a book. If I could do that I would be happy."

I wondered. The book in question had only seemed to me good in spots and the spots had been far apart. There was too much depen-

[1] Written 1924. Published in *The Literary Review.*

dence upon the notebook. The writer had seemed to me to have very little to give out of himself. What had happened, I thought, was that the writer of the book had confused the life of reality with the life of the fancy. Easy enough to get a thrill out of people with reality. A man struck by an automobile, a child falling out at the window of a city office building. Such things stir the emotions. No one, however, confuses them with art.

This confusion of the life of the imagination with the life of reality is a trap into which most of our critics seem to me to fall about a dozen times each year. Do the trick over and over and in they tumble. "It is life," they say. "Another great artist has been discovered."

What never seems to come quite clear is the simple fact that art is art. It is not life.

The life of the imagination will always remain separated from the life of reality. It feeds upon the life of reality, but it is not that life—cannot be. Mr. John Marin painting Brooklyn Bridge, Henry Fielding writing *Tom Jones*, are not trying in the novel and the painting to give us reality. They are striving for a realization in art of something out of their own imaginative experiences, fed to be sure upon the life immediately about. A quite different matter from making an actual picture of what they see before them.

And here arises a confusion. For some reason—I myself have never exactly understood very clearly—the imagination must constantly feed upon reality or starve. Separate yourself too much from life and you may at moments be a lyrical poet, but you are not an artist. Something within dries up, starves for the want of food. Upon the fact in nature the imagination must constantly feed in order that the imaginative life remain significant. The workman who lets his imagination drift off into some experience altogether disconnected with reality, the attempt of the American to depict life in Europe, the New Englander writing of cowboy life—all that sort of thing—in ninety-nine cases out of a hundred ends in the work of such a man becoming at once full of holes and bad spots. The intelligent reader, tricked often enough by the technical skill displayed in hiding the holes, never in the end accepts it as good work. The imagination of the workman has become confused. He has had to depend altogether upon tricks. The whole job is a fake.

The difficulty, I fancy, is that so few workmen in the arts will accept their own limitations. It is only when the limitation is fully accepted that it ceases to be a limitation. Such men scold at the life immediately about. "It's too dull and commonplace to make good material," they declare. Off they sail in fancy to the

 South Seas, to Africa, to China. What they cannot realize is their own dullness. Life is never dull except to the dull.

The writer who sets himself down to write a tale has undertaken something. He has undertaken to conduct his readers on a trip through the world of his fancy. If he is a novelist his imaginative world is filled with people and events. If he have any sense of decency as a workman he can no more tell lies about his imagined people, fake them, than he can sell out real people in real life. The thing is constantly done but no man I have ever met, having done such a trick, has felt very clean about the matter afterward.

On the other hand, when the writer is rather intensely true to the people of his imaginative world, when he has set them down truly, when he does not fake, another confusion arises. Being square with your people in the imaginative world does not mean lifting them over into life, into reality. There is a very subtle distinction to be made and upon the writer's ability to make this distinction will in the long run depend his standing as a workman.

Having lifted the reader out of the reality of daily life it is entirely possible for the writer to do his job so well that the imaginative life becomes to the reader for the time real life. Little real touches are added. The people of the

town—that never existed except in the fancy— 
eat food, live in houses, suffer, have moments of happiness and die. To the writer, as he works, they are very real. The imaginative world in which he is for the time living has become for him more alive than the world of reality ever can become. His very sincerity confuses. Being unversed in the matter of making the delicate distinction, that the writer himself sometimes has such a hard time making, they call him a realist. The notion shocks him. "The deuce, I am nothing of the kind," he says. "But such a thing could not have happened in a Vermont town." "Why not? Have you not learned that anything can happen anywhere? If a thing can happen in my imaginative world it can of course happen in the flesh and blood world. Upon what do you fancy my imagination feeds?"

My own belief is that the writer with a note-book in his hand is always a bad workman, a man who distrusts his own imagination. Such a man describes actual scenes accurately, he puts down actual conversation.

But people do not converse in the book world as they do in life. Scenes of the imaginative world are not real scenes.

The life of reality is confused, disorderly, almost always without apparent purpose, whereas in the artist's imaginative life there is purpose. There is determination to give the tale, the song, the painting Form—to make it true and real to the theme, not to life. Often the better the job is done the greater the confusion.

I myself remember with what a shock I heard people say that one of my own books, *Winesburg, Ohio*, was an exact picture of Ohio village life. The book was written in a crowded tenement district of Chicago. The hint for almost every character was taken from my fellow-lodgers in a large rooming house, many of whom had never lived in a village. The confusion arises out of the fact that others besides practicing artists have imaginations. But most people are afraid to trust their imaginations and the artist is not.

Would it not be better to have it understood that realism, in so far as the word means reality to life, is always bad art—although it may possibly be very good journalism?

Which is but another way of saying that all of the so-called great realists were not realists at all and never intended being. Madame Bovary did not exist in fact. She existed in the imaginative life of Flaubert and he managed to make her exist also in the imaginative life of his readers.

. . . . . .

I have been writing a story. A man is walking in a street and suddenly turns out of the street into an alleyway. There he meets another man and a hurried whispered conversation takes place. In real life they may be but a pair of rather small bootleggers, but they are not that to me.

When I began writing, the physical aspect of one of the men, the one who walked in the street, was taken rather literally from life. He looked strikingly like a man I once knew, so much like him in fact that there was a confusion. A matter easy enough to correct.

A stroke of my pen saves me from realism. The man I knew in life had red hair; he was tall and thin.

With a few words I have changed him completely. Now he has black hair and a black mustache. He is short and has broad shoulders. And now he no longer lives in the world of reality. He is a denizen of my own imaginative world. He can now begin a life having nothing at all to do with the life of the red-haired man.

If I am to succeed in making him real in this new world he, like hundreds of other men and women who live only in my own fanciful world, must live and move within the scope of the story or novel into which I have cast him. If I do tricks with him in the imaginative world, sell him out, I become merely a romancer. If, however, I have the courage to let him really live he will, perhaps, show me the way to a fine story or novel.

But the story or novel will not be a picture of life. I will never have had any intention of making it that.

# AFTER SEEING GEORGE BELLOWS' MR. AND MRS. WASE

## AFTER SEEING GEORGE BELLOWS' MR. AND MRS. WASE

THE parrot bothered me at first and then the book she holds in her hand. The book may be a Bible. Later I understood about the parrot. Mrs. Wase's sister sent it to her from Florida. She was a Freer and when her husband got killed she got his life insurance. She went to Florida one winter and sent the parrot home to Martha. When she was down there they tried to sell her an orange grove, but she knew how to hang onto her money. The real estate agent was pretty slick. He could talk.



The Freer boys like games of all kinds and Ike Freer got to be a baseball pitcher. He was in the Texas League once, with Fort Worth, but his arm went bad on him.

He's a house painter now.

Mr. Wase is an engineer on the Wheeling Railroad, a road that goes from Wheeling, West Virginia, to Toledo, Ohio, and carries coal mostly.

The Wases had one boy, Ed Wase. He was a good boy, but he got killed in the war. It seemed to draw Mr. and Mrs. Wase closer to each other, but Mrs. Wase hasn't ever been the same woman since it happened. You can't hardly get her to look on the cheerful side of things much.

The relation between the artist and the workman is very subtle and difficult to define. Some artists feel it, others do not. There are artists who would like to deny it. They would like to think of themselves as aristocrats.

What a notion! The artist must work with his hands. He must feel within himself some deep relationship between himself, as a man, and the world of nature, of materials.

The earth in which men have always plowed and planted, trees, stones lying in fields, seas breaking on shores, a world filled with materials out of which he is to try to create something with his hands.

Workingmen also express themselves through their hands. Look at the hands of Mr. and Mrs. Wase. Years of touching things, doing things. The fingers, in the end, often become more alive than all the rest of the body.

Looking at this painting you get a new feeling about Mr. George Bellows. I myself did not know the man well, only met him once or twice, quite casually. He must have had in him that quality of masculine tenderness that is so rare and precious. It expresses itself, in a man, in the way he touches things, what it means to him to touch things—life in trees, in stones, color, materials of all sorts.

The arts are always being swept here and there by movements. It would be so satisfactory to us all if we could get the arts defined, if there were only some definite rule or formula by which, when we stand before a work of art, we could say "this is good or that is bad." Workmen in stone, in color, in sound, in words are always being bothered by the same desire. Mr. George Bellows must always have been on the hunt, trying one approach and then another. He died too soon. There are few enough such men.

My notion is that we would all chuck all of the arts out of our lives if we could. They are such a bother. The challenge is always there. "Get a little closer. Give more of yourself. Be more impersonal. Love more."

"Love what?"

Well, say this life in which we all live. That's something, isn't it? Life as it is in stones, trees, skies, seas, people, too.

Few enough people realize that all art that has vitality must have its basis in love. You see women sometimes of whom it might be said that they find direct and simple expression of the need for giving love in their relations with people about them, but with men that is somewhat difficult. It may be impossible. It may be that men are intended primarily to be workmen, that they must find an outlet for the inner needs in their work or they will not find it at all.

As for myself I find an expression of all I am trying to say here in this painting by Mr. Bellows. Men are seldom so tender, so understanding, so cleanly courageous as Mr. Bellows must have been when he faced this canvas. You get back to the people painted by Mr. Bellows and forget him and that is as it should be. That is what the artist intends and wants when he is really feeling the thing on which he is at work.

Mr. Wase going to his job every day. When he isn't at work he thinks of his job. There are ways to get by with a job, but that isn't enough. You want to do it a little better and a little better and a little better. Life is short, after all. You just begin to learn a little something and then you die. What you realize, what every man dimly realizes, is that what a man feels toward his work, he is. We have all in the end got to square ourselves with ourselves if we can.

The challenge is always there. "Get a little closer. Give more of yourself. Be more impersonal before the possibilities of the materials you touch with your fingers. Love more."

AFTER SEEING GEORGE BELLOWS' MR. AND MRS. WASE.

Mr. and Mrs. Wase, both in their dumb way, keep telling you things. They are telling you that Mr. George Bellows died too young. They are telling you that he was after something, that he was always after it.

# I'LL SAY WE'VE DONE WELL

# I'LL SAY WE'VE DONE WELL[1]

## FOREWORD



I AM compelled to write of the State of Ohio reminiscently and from flashing impressions got during these last ten years, although I was born there, spent my young manhood within its borders, and later went back and spent another five or six years as a manufacturer in the State. And so I have always thought of myself as an Ohioan and no doubt shall always remain, inside myself, an Ohioan.

Very well, then, it is my State and there are a thousand things within it I love and as many things I do not like much at all. And I dare say I might have some difficulty setting down just the things about Ohio that I most dislike were it not for the fact that what I am to write is to appear in *The Nation*, and *The Nation*, being—well, anyway, what they call broad-minded, cannot well refuse room to my particular form of broadening out, as it were.

[1] Written 1922. Published in *The Nation*. Part of a series of articles on States of the Union.

I'LL SAY WE'VE DONE WELL.

Ohio is a big State. It is strong. It is the State of Harding and McKinley. I am told that my own father once played in the Silver Cornet Band at Caledonia, Ohio. Warren G. might have remembered him as Teddy, sometimes called Major Anderson. He ran a small harness shop at Caledonia. Just why he was called Major I never knew. Perhaps because his people came from the South. Anyway, I ought to have got a job at Washington. Everyone else from that county did.

And now Ohio has got very big and very strong and its Youngstown, Cincinnati, Akron, Cleveland, Toledo, and perhaps a dozen other prosperous industrial cities, can put themselves forward as being as ugly, as noisy, as dirty, and as careless in their civic spirit as any American industrial cities anywhere. "Come you men of 'these States,'" as old Walt Whitman was so fond of saying, in his windier moods, trot out your cities. Have you a city that smells worse than Akron, that is a worse junk-heap of ugliness than Youngstown, that is more smugly self-satisfied than Cleveland, or that has missed as unbelievably great an opportunity to be one of the lovely cities of the world as has the city of Cincinnati? I'll warrant you have not. In this modern pushing American civilization of ours you other States have nothing on our Ohio. Credit where credit is due, citizens. I claim that we Ohio men have taken as lovely a land as ever lay outdoors and that we have, in our towns and cities, put the old stamp of ourselves on it for keeps.

I'LL SAY WE'VE DONE WELL.

Of course, you understand, that to do this we have had to work. Take, for example, a city like Cincinnati. There it sits on its hills, the lovely southern Ohio and northern Kentucky hills, and a poet coming there might have gone into the neighboring hills and looked down on the site of the great city; well, what I say is that such a poet might have dreamed of a white and golden city nestling there with the beautiful Ohio at its feet. And that city might, you understand, have crept off into the green hills, that the poet might have compared to the breasts of goddesses, and in the morning when the sun came out and the men, women, and children of the city came out of their houses and looking abroad over the sweet land of Ohio——

But pshaw, let's cut that bunk.

We Ohioans tackled the job and we put the kibosh on that poet tribe for keeps. If you don't believe it, go down and look at our city of Cincinnati now. We have done something against great odds down there. First, we had to lick the poet out of our own hearts and then we had to lick nature herself, but we did it. Today our river front in Cincinnati is as mean looking a place as the lake front in Chicago or

I'LL SAY WE'VE DONE WELL.

Cleveland, and you please bear in mind that down there in Cincinnati we had less money to work with than they did up in Chicago or even in Cleveland.

Well, we did it. We have ripped up those hills and cut out all that breasts-of-goddesses stuff and we've got a whanging big Rotary Club and a few years ago we won the World Series, or bought it, and we've got some nice rotten old boats in the river and some old sheds on the waterfront where, but for us, there might not have been anything but water.

And now let's move about the State a little while I point out to you a few more things we have done. Of course we haven't any Henry Ford over there, but just bear in mind that John D. Rockefeller and Mark Hanna and Harvey Firestone and Willys up at Toledo and a lot of other live ones are Ohio men and what I claim is—they have done well.

Look at what we had to buck up against. You go back into American history a little and you'll see for yourself what I mean. Do you remember when La Salle was working his way westward, up there in Canada, and he kept hearing about a country to the south and a river called the Ohio? The rest of his crowd didn't want to go down that way and so, being a modest man and not wanting to set himself up against public opinion, he pretended to be down of a bad sickness. So the rest of the lot, priests and Indians and others, went on out west and he just took a couple of years off and cut out southward alone, with a few Indians. And even afoot and through the thick woods a man can cover quite a considerable amount of territory in two years. My notion is he probably saw it all.

I'LL SAY WE'VE DONE WELL.

I remember that an old man I knew when I was a boy told me about seeing the Ohio River in the early days, when the rolling hills along its banks were still covered with great trees, and what he said I can't remember exactly, but anyway, he gave me the impression of a sweet, clear and majestic stream, in which a man could swim and see the sand of the bottom far below, through the sparkling water. The impression I got from the old man was of boys swimming on their backs, white clouds floating overhead, the hills running away and the branches of trees tossed by the wind like the waves of a vast green sea.

It may be that La Salle went there and did that. It wouldn't surprise me if some such scandal should creep out about him. And then, maybe, after he got down to where Louisville, Kentucky, now stands, and he found he couldn't get any further with his boats because of the falls in the river—or pretended he couldn't because he was so stuck on the fine Ohio country up above—it may be, I say, that he turned back and went northward along eastern Ohio and into a land of even more majestic hills and finer forests and got finally into that country of soft-stepping little hills, up there facing Lake Erie.

I say maybe he did and I have my own reasons. You see this fellow La Salle wasn't much of a one to talk. He didn't advertise very well. What I mean is he was an uncommunicative man. But you go look him up in the books and you will see that later he was always being condemned, after that trip, and that he was always afterward accused of being a visionary and a dreamer.

From all I've ever been able to hear about Ohio, as it was before we white men and New Englanders got in there and went to work, the land might have done that to La Salle, and for that matter to our own sons too, if we, God-fearing men, hadn't got in there just when we did, and rolled up our sleeves and got right down to the business of making a good, up-and-coming, Middle-Western American State out of it. And, thank goodness, we had the old pep in us to do it. We original northern Ohio men were mostly New Englanders and we came out of cold, stony New England and over the rocky hills of northern New York State to get into Ohio.

I suppose the hardship we endured before we

got to Ohio was what helped us to bang right ahead and cut down trees and build railroads and whang the Indians over the heads with our picks and shovels and put up churches and later start the Anti-saloon League and all the other splendid things we have done. I'll tell you what the country makes no mistake when it comes to our State for Presidents. We train our sons up right over there.

I'LL SAY WE'VE DONE WELL.

Why, I can remember myself, when I was a boy, and how I once got out of a job and went one fall with a string of race horses all over our State. I found out then what La Salle was up against when our State was what you might call new, in a way of speaking. Why, I got as dreamy and mopy, drifting along through the beautiful Ohio country that fall, as any no-account you ever saw. I fooled along until I got fired. That's how I came out.

Then, of course, I had to go into the cities and get a job in a factory and the better way of life got in its chance at me, so that for years I had as good a bringing up and knew as much about hustling and pushing myself forward and advertising and not getting dreamy or visionary as any American there is. What I mean is that if I have slipped any since I do not blame the modern Ohio people for it. It's my own fault. You can't blame a town like Toledo or Cleve-

I'LL SAY WE'VE DONE WELL.

land or Akron or any of our up-and-coming Ohio cities if a man turns out to be a bum American and doesn't care about driving a motor at fifty miles an hour or doesn't go to the movies much evenings.

What I mean to say is that this business of writing up the States in the pages of *The Nation* is, I'll bet anything, going to turn out just as I expected. There'll be a lot of knocking, that's what I'll bet. But I'm not going to do that. I live in Chicago now and our motto out here is, "Put away your hammer and get out your horn." Mayor Thompson of Chicago got that up. And, anyway, I think it is pretty much all silliness, this knocking and this carping criticism of everything American and splendid I hear going on nowadays. I'm that way myself sometimes and I'm ashamed of it.

The trouble with me is that I once had a perfectly good little factory over in Ohio, and there was a nice ash-heap in a vacant lot beside it, and it was on a nice stream, and I dumped stuff out of my factory and killed the fish in it and spoiled it just splendid for a while. What I think now is that I would have been all right and a good man too, but on summer afternoons I got to moping about the Ohio hills alone, instead of going over to the Elks Club and playing pool where I might have got in with some of the boys and picked up some good points. There were a lot of good bang-up Ohio pushers over in that Ohio town I had my factory in and I neglected them. So, of course, I went broke and I'll admit I've been rather a sorehead ever since. But when I come down to admit the honest truth I'll have to say it wasn't Ohio's fault at all.

I'LL SAY WE'VE DONE WELL.

Why, do you know, I've had times when I thought I'd like to see that strip of country we call Ohio, just as that Frenchman La Salle must have seen it. What I mean is with nothing over there but the dear green hills and the clear sweet rivers and nobody around but a few Indians and all the whites and the splendid modern cities all gone to—I won't say where because it's a thought I don't have very often and I'm ashamed of it.

What I suppose gets me yet is what got me when I stayed away from the Elks Club and went walking in the hills when I was trying to be a manufacturer, and what got me fired when I was a race-track swipe. I get to thinking of what that darned old man once told me. I'll bet he was a Bolshevik. What he told me set me dreaming about swimming in clear streams, and seeing white cities sitting on hills, and of other cities up along the northern end of my State, facing Lake Erie, where in the evening canoes and maybe even gondolas would drift in and out of the lake and among the stone houses, whose color was slowly changing and growing richer with the passage of time.

But, as I say, that's all poet stuff and bunk. Having such pipe dreams is just what put the old kibosh on my factory, I'll bet anything. What I think is that a man should be glad it's getting harder and harder for any of our sons to make the same mistakes I did. For, as I figure it out, things are going just splendidly over in Ohio now. Why, nearly every town is a factory town now and some of them have got streets in them that would make New York or London or Chicago sit up and take notice. What I mean is, almost as many people to every square foot of ground and just as jammed up and dirty and smoky.

To be sure, the job isn't all done yet. There are lots of places where you can still see the green hills and every once in a while a citizen of a city like Cleveland, for example, gets a kind of accidental glimpse at the lake, but even in a big town like Chicago, where they have a lot of money and a large police force, a thing like that will happen now and then. You can't do everything all at once. But things are getting better all the time. A little more push, a little more old zip and go, and a man over in Ohio can lead a decent life.

He can get up in the morning and go through a street where all the houses are nicely blacked up with coal soot, and into a factory where all he has to do all day long is to drill a hole in a piece of iron. It's fine the way Ford and Willys and all such fellows have made factory work so nice. Nowadays all you have to do, if you live in an up-to-date Ohio town, is to make, say, twenty-three million holes in pieces of iron, all just alike, in a lifetime. Isn't that fine? And at night a fellow can go home thanking God, and he can walk right past the finest cinder piles and places where they dump old tin cans and everything without paying a cent.

I'LL SAY WE'VE DONE WELL.

And so I don't see why what such cities as Cleveland and Cincinnati have done to knock dreaminess and natural beauty of scene galley-west can't be done also by all the smaller towns and cities pretty fast now. What I'm sure is they can do it if the old New England stock hasn't worn out and if they keep out foreign influences all they can. And even the farmers can make their places out in the country look more modern and like the slums of a good live city like Chicago or Cleveland if they'll only pep up and work a little harder this fall when the crops are laid by.

And so, as far as I can see, what I say is, Ohio is O.K.

# A MEETING SOUTH

# A MEETING SOUTH [1]

A MEETING SOUTH.

He told me the story of his ill fortune with a very gentlemanly little smile on his very sensitive lips. Such things happened. He might well have been speaking of another. I liked his tone, liked him.

This happened in New Orleans, where I had gone to live. When he came, Fred, for whom he was looking, had gone away, but immediately I felt a strong desire to know him better and so suggested we spend the evening together. When we went down the stairs I noticed that he was a cripple. The slight limp, the look of pain that occasionally drifted across his face, the little laugh that was intended to be jolly, but did not quite achieve its purpose, all these things began at once to tell me the story I have now set myself down to write.

"I shall take him to see Aunt Sally," I thought. One does not take every chance caller to Aunt Sally. However when she is in fine feather, when she has taken a fancy to her visitor, there is no one like her. Although she

[1] Written in 1924. Published in *Dial*, 1925.

has lived in New Orleans for thirty years, Aunt Sally is Middle-Western, born and bred.

However I am plunging a bit too abruptly into my story.

First of all I must speak more of my guest and for convenience's sake I shall call him David. I felt at once that he would be wanting a drink and such things can be managed. We achieved several and my own head became somewhat shaky, but I could see that what we had taken had not affected him. Evening was coming, the abrupt waning of the day and the quick smoky soft-footed coming of night characteristic of our semi-tropic city, when he produced a bottle from his hip pocket. It was so large that I was amazed. How had it happened that the carrying of so large a bottle had not made him look deformed? His body was very small and delicately built. "Perhaps, like the kangaroo, his body has developed some kind of a natural pouch for taking care of supplies," I thought. Really he walked as one might fancy a kangaroo would walk when out for a quiet evening stroll. I went along thinking of Darwin and the marvels of prohibition. "We are a wonderful people, we Americans," I thought. We were both in fine humor, had begun to like each other immensely.

He explained the bottle. The stuff, he said, was made by a nigger on his father's plantation somewhere over in Alabama. We sat on the steps of a vacant house deep down in the old French Quarter of New Orleans—the Vieux Carre—while he explained that his father had no intention of breaking the law—that is to say, in so far as the law remained reasonable. "Our nigger just makes whisky for us," he said. "We keep him for that purpose. He doesn't have anything else to do, just makes the family whisky, that's all. If he went selling any we'd raise hell with him. I dare say Dad would shoot him if he caught him up to any such unlawful trick, and you bet, Jim, our nigger I'm telling you of, knows it too."

"He's a good whisky maker though, don't you think?" David added. He talked of Jim in a warm friendly way. "Lord he's been with us always, was born with us. His wife cooks for us and Jim makes our whisky. It's a race to see which is best at their job, but I think Jim will win. He's getting a little better all the time and all of our family—well I guess we just like and need our whisky more than we do our food."

Do you know Orleans? Have you lived there in the summer when it is hot, in the winter when it rains, and through the glorious late falls? Its own people scorn it now. In New Orleans there is a sense of shame because the city is not more like Chicago or Pittsburgh.

It however suited David and me. We walked,

slowly, on account of his bad leg, through many streets of the Old Town, negro women laughing all around us in the dusk, shadows playing over old buildings, children with their shrill cries dodging in and out of old hallways. The old city was once almost altogether French, but now it is becoming more and more Italian. It however remains Latin. People live out of doors. Families were sitting down to dinner within full sight of the street—all doors and windows open. A man and his wife quarreled in Italian. In a patio back of an old building a negress sang a French song.

We came out of the narrow little streets and had a drink in front of the dark cathedral and another in a little square in front. There is a statue of General Jackson, always taking off his hat to Northern tourists who in the winter come down to see the city. At his horse's feet an inscription—"The Union must and will be preserved." We drank solemnly to that declaration and the general seemed to bow a bit lower. "He was sure a proud man," David said as we went over toward the docks to sit in the darkness and look at the Mississippi. All good New Orleansians go to look at the Mississippi at least once a day. At night it is like creeping into a dark bedroom to look at a sleeping child—something of that sort—gives you the same warm nice feeling I mean. David is a poet and so in the darkness by the river we spoke of Keats and Shelley, the two English poets all good Southern men love.

All of this, you are to understand, was before I took him to see Aunt Sally.

Both Aunt Sally and myself are Middle-Westerners. We are but guests down here, but perhaps we shall both stay here until we die. Something of the sort is in the wind. I don't quite know how it has happened.

A great many Northern men and women come down our way and when they go back North write things about the South. The trick is to write nigger stories. The North likes them. They are so amusing. One of the best known writers of nigger stories was down here recently and a man I know, a Southern man, went to call on him. The writer seemed a bit nervous. "I don't know much about the South or Southerners," he said. "But you have your reputation," my friend said. The writer had a notion he was being made sport of. "Now look here," he said, "I don't claim to be no highbrow. I'm a business man myself. At home, up North, I associate mostly with business men and when I am not at work I go out to the country club. I want you to understand I am not setting myself up." My friend said he appeared angry. "About what now, do you fancy?" he asked innocently.

However, I am not thinking of the Northern writer of negro stories. I am thinking of the Southern poet, with the bottle clasped firmly in his hands, sitting in the darkness beside me on the docks facing the Mississippi.

He spoke at some length of his gift for drinking. "I didn't always have it. It is a thing built up," he said. The story of how he chanced to be a cripple came out slowly. You are to remember that my own head was a bit unsteady. In the darkness the river, very deep and very powerful off New Orleans, was creeping away to the gulf. The whole river seemed to move away from us and then to slip noiselessly into the darkness like a vast moving sidewalk.

When he had first come to me, in the late afternoon, and when we had started for our walk together I had noticed that one of his legs dragged as we went along and that he kept putting a thin hand to an equally thin cheek.

Sitting over by the river he explained as a boy would explain that he had stubbed his toe running down a hill.

When the World War broke out he went over to England and managed to get himself enrolled as an aviator, very much, I gathered, in the spirit in which a countryman, in a city for a night, might take in a show.

The English had been glad enough to take

him on. He was one more man. They were glad enough to take any one on just then. He was small and delicately built, but after he got in he turned out to be a first rate flyer, serving all through the war with a British flying squadron, but at the last got into a crash and fell.

Both legs were broken, one of them in three places, the scalp was badly torn and some of the bones of the face had been splintered.

They had put him into a field hospital and had patched him up. "It was my fault if the job was rather bungled," he said. "You see it was a field hospital, a hell of a place. Men were torn all to pieces, groaning and dying. Then they moved me back to a base hospital and it wasn't much better. The fellow who had the bed next to mine had shot himself in the foot to avoid going into a battle. A lot of them did that, but why they picked on their own feet that way is beyond me. It's a nasty place, full of small bones. If you're ever going to shoot yourself don't pick on a spot like that. Don't pick on your feet. I tell you it's a bad idea.

"Anyway the man in the hospital was always making a fuss and I got sick of him and the place too. When I got better I faked, said the nerves of my leg didn't hurt, said the nerves up in my face didn't hurt. It was a lie of course. The nerves of my leg and of my face have never quit hurting. I guess maybe, if I had told the truth, they might have fixed me up all right."

I got it. No wonder he carried his drinks so well. When I understood I wanted to keep on drinking with him, wanted to stay with him until he got tired of me as he had of the man who lay beside him in the base hospital over there somewhere in France.

The point was that he never slept, could not sleep, except when he was a little drunk. "I'm a nut," he said smiling.

It was after we got over to Aunt Sally's that he talked most. Aunt Sally had gone to bed when we got there, but she got up when we rang the bell and we all went to sit together in the little patio back of her house. She is a large woman with great arms and rather a paunch and she had put on nothing but a light flowered dressing gown over a thin, ridiculously girlish, nightgown. By this time the moon had come up and, outside, in the narrow street of the Vieux Carre, three drunken sailors from a ship in the river were sitting on a curb and singing a song,

"I've got to get it,
You've got to get it,
We've all got to get it
In our own good time."

They had rather nice boyish voices and every time they sang a verse and had done the chorus they all laughed together heartily.



In Aunt Sally's patio there are many broad-leafed banana plants and a Chinaberry tree throwing their soft purple shadows on a brick floor.

As for Aunt Sally, she is as strange to me as he was. When we came and when we were all seated at a little table in the patio, she ran into her house and presently came back with a bottle of whisky. She, it seemed, had understood him at once, had understood without unnecessary words that the little Southern man lived always in the black house of pain, that whisky was good to him, that it quieted his throbbing nerves, temporarily at least. "Everything is temporary when you come to that," I can fancy Aunt Sally saying.

We sat for a time in silence, David having shifted his allegiance and taken two drinks out of Aunt Sally's bottle. Presently he arose and walked up and down the patio floor, crossing and recrossing the network of delicately outlined shadows on the bricks. "It's really all right, the leg," he said, "something just presses on the nerves, that's all." In me there was a self-satisfied feeling. I had done the right thing. I had brought him to Aunt Sally. "I have brought him to a mother." She has always made me feel that way since I have known her.

And now I shall have to explain her a little. It will not be so easy. Our whole neighborhood is alive with tales concerning her.

Aunt Sally came to New Orleans in the old days, when the town was alive, in the wide-open days. What she had been before she came here no one knows, but anyway she opened a place. That was very, very long ago when I was myself but a lad, up in Ohio. As I have already said Aunt Sally came from somewhere up in the Middle-Western country. In some obscure subtle way it would flatter me to think she came from my state.

The house she had opened was one of the older places in the French Quarter down here, and when she had got her hands on it Aunt Sally had a hunch. Instead of making the place modern, cutting it up into small rooms, all that sort of thing, she left it just as it was and spent her money in rebuilding falling old walls, mending winding broad old stairways, repairing dim high-ceilinged old rooms, soft-colored old marble mantels. After all we do seem attached to sin and there are so many people busy making sin unattractive. It is good to find someone who takes the other road. It would have been so very much to Aunt Sally's advantage to have made the place modern, that is to say, in the business she was in at that time. If a few old rooms, wide old stairways, old cooking ovens built into the walls, if all these things did not facilitate the stealing in of couples on dark nights they at least did something else. She had opened a gambling and drinking house, but one can have no doubt about the ladies stealing in. "I was on the make all right," Aunt Sally told me once.

She ran the place and took in money and the money she spent on the place itself. A falling wall was made to stand up straight and fine again, the banana plants were made to grow in the patio, the Chinaberry tree got started and was helped through the years of adolescence. On the wall the lovely Rose of Montana bloomed madly. The fragrant Lantana grew in a dense mass at a corner of the wall.

When the Chinaberry tree, planted at the very center of the patio, began to get up into the light it filled the whole neighborhood with fragrance in the spring.

Fifteen, twenty years of that, with Mississippi River gamblers and racehorse men sitting at tables by windows in the huge rooms upstairs in the house that had once, no doubt, been the town house of some rich planter's family—in the boom days of the 'forties. Women stealing in, too, in the dusk of evenings. Drinks being sold. Aunt Sally raking down the kitty from the game, raking in her share, quite ruthlessly.

At night getting a good price too from the lovers. No questions asked, a good price for drinks. Moll Flanders might have lived with Aunt Sally. What a pair they would have made. The Chinaberry tree beginning to be lusty. The Lantana blossoming—in the fall the Rose of Montana.

Aunt Sally getting hers. Using the money to keep the old house in fine shape. Salting some away all the time.

A motherly soul, good, sensible Middle-Western woman, eh? Once a racehorse man left twenty-four thousand dollars with her and disappeared. No one knew she had it. There was a report the man was dead. He had killed a gambler in a place down by the French Market and while they were looking for him he managed to slip in to Aunt Sally's and leave his swag. Sometime later a body was found floating in the river and it was identified as the horseman, but in reality he had been picked up in a wire-tapping haul in New York City and did not get out of his Northern prison for six years.

When he did get out naturally he skipped for New Orleans. No doubt he was somewhat shaky. She had him. If he squealed there was the murder charge to be brought up and held over his head. It was night when he arrived and Aunt Sally went at once to an old brick oven built into the wall of the kitchen and took out a bag. "There it is," she said. The whole affair was a part of the day's work for her in those days.

A MEETING SOUTH.

Gamblers at the tables in some of the rooms upstairs—lurking couples—from the old patio below the fragrance of growing things.

When she was fifty Aunt Sally had got enough and had put them all out. She did not stay in the way of sin too long and she never went in too deep, like that Moll Flanders, and so she was all right and sitting pretty. "They wanted to gamble and drink and play with the ladies. The ladies liked it all right. I never saw none of them come in protesting too much. The worst was in the morning when they went away. They looked so sheepish and guilty. If they felt that way what made them come? If I took to a man you bet I'd want him and no monkey business or nothing doing.

"I got a little tired of all of them, that's the truth." Aunt Sally laughed. "But that wasn't until I had got what I went after. Oh, pshaw, they took up too much of my time after I got enough to be safe."

Aunt Sally is now sixty-five. If you like her and she likes you she will let you sit with her in her patio gossiping of the old times, of the old river days. Perhaps—well you see there is still something of the French influence at work in New Orleans, a sort of matter-of-factness about life—what I started to say is that if you know Aunt Sally and she likes you, and if, by chance, your lady likes the smell of flowers growing in a patio at night— Really I am going a bit too far. I only meant to suggest that Aunt Sally at sixty-five is not harsh. She is a motherly soul.

We sat in the garden talking, the little Southern poet, Aunt Sally, and myself—or rather they talked and I listened. The Southerner's great grandfather was English, a younger son, and he came over here to make his fortune as a planter and did it. Once he and his sons owned several great plantations with slaves, but now his father had but a few hundred acres left, about one of the old houses—somewhere over in Alabama. The land is heavily mortgaged and most of it has not been under cultivation for years. Negro labor is growing more and more expensive and unsatisfactory since so many negroes have run off to Chicago, and the poet's father and the one brother at home are not much good at working the land. "We aren't strong enough and we don't know how," the poet said.

The Southerner had come to New Orleans to see Fred, to talk with Fred about poetry, but Fred was out of town. I could but walk about with him, help him drink his home-made whisky. Already I had taken nearly a dozen drinks. In the morning I would have a headache.

I drew within myself, listening while David and Aunt Sally talked. The Chinaberry tree had been so and so many years growing—she spoke of it as she might have spoken of a daughter. "It had a lot of different sicknesses when it was young, but it pulled through." Someone had built a high wall on one side her patio so that the climbing plants did not get as much sunlight as they needed. The banana plants however did very well and now the Chinaberry tree was big and strong enough to take care of itself. She kept giving David drinks of whisky and he talked.

He told her of the place in his leg where something, a bone, perhaps, pressed on the nerve, and of the place on his left cheek. A silver plate had been set under the skin. She touched the spot with her fat old fingers. The moonlight fell softly down on the patio floor. "I can't sleep except somewhere out of doors," David said.

He explained how that, at home on his father's plantation, he had to be thinking all day of whether or not he would be able to sleep at night.

"I go to bed and then I get up. There is

always a bottle of whisky on the table downstairs and I take three or four drinks. Then I go out doors." Often very nice things happened.

"In the fall it's best," he said. "You see the niggers are making molasses." Every negro cabin on the place had a little clump of ground back of it where cane grew and in the fall the negroes were making their 'lasses. "I take the bottle in my hand and go into the fields, unseen by the niggers. Having the bottle with me, that way, I drink a good deal and then lie down on the ground. The mosquitoes bite me some, but I don't mind much. I reckon I get drunk enough not to mind. The little pain makes a kind of rhythm for the bigger pain—like poetry.

"In a kind of shed the niggers are making the 'lasses, that is to say pressing the juice out of the cane and boiling it down. They keep singing as they work. In a few years now I reckon our family won't have any land. The banks could take it now if they wanted it. They don't want it. It would be too much trouble for them to manage I reckon.

"In the fall, at night, the niggers are pressing the cane. Our niggers live pretty much on 'lasses and grits.

"They like working at night and I'm glad they do. There is an old mule going round and round in a circle and beside the press a pile of the dry cane. Niggers come, men and women, old and young. They build a fire outside the shed. The old mule goes round and round.



"The niggers sing. They laugh and shout. Sometimes the young niggers with their gals make love on the dry cane pile. I can hear it rattle.

"I have come out of the big house, me and my bottle, and I creep along, low on the ground, 'til I get up close. There I lie. I'm a little drunk. It all makes me happy. I can sleep some, on the ground like that, when the niggers are singing, when no one knows I'm there. I don't know. Maybe they do know I'm there.

"I could sleep here, on these bricks here," David said, pointing to where the shadows cast by the broad leaves of the banana plants were broadest and deepest.

He got up from his chair and went limping, dragging one foot after the other, across the patio and lay down on the bricks.

For a long time Aunt Sally and I sat looking at each other, saying nothing, and presently she made a sign with her fat finger and we crept away into the house. "I'll let you out at the front door. You let him sleep, right where he is," she said. In spite of her huge bulk and her age she had walked across the patio floor as softly as a kitten. Beside her I felt awkward and uncertain. When we had got inside she whispered to me. She had some champagne left from the old days, hidden away somewhere in the old house. "I'm going to send a magnum up to his dad when he goes home," she explained.

She, it seemed, was very happy, having him there, drunk and asleep on the brick floor of the patio. "We used to have some good men come here in the old days too," she said. As we went into the house through the kitchen door I had looked back at David, asleep now in the heavy shadows at a corner of the wall. There was no doubt he also was happy, had been happy ever since I had brought him into the presence of Aunt Sally. What a small huddled figure of a man he looked, lying thus on the brick, under the night sky, in the deep shadows of the banana plants.

I went into the house and out at the front door and into a dark narrow street thinking. Well, I was after all a Northern man. It was possible Aunt Sally had become completely Southern, being down here so long.

I remembered that it was the chief boast of her life that once she had shaken hands with John L. Sullivan and that she had known P. T. Barnum. "We were friends once," she said with a touch of pride in her voice, speaking of Barnum. "I knew Dave Gears. You mean to tell me you don't know who Dave Gears was? Why he was one of the biggest gamblers we ever had in this city."

As for David and his poetry—it is in the manner of Shelley. "If I could write like Shelley I would be happy. I wouldn't care what happened to me," he had said during our walk of the early part of the evening.

I went along enjoying my thoughts. The street was dark and occasionally I laughed. A notion had come to me. It kept dancing in my head and I thought it very delicious. It had something to do with aristocrats, with such people as Aunt Sally and David. "Lordy," I thought, "maybe I do understand them a little. I'm from the Middle-West myself and it seems we can produce our aristocrats too. I kept thinking of Aunt Sally and of my native state of Ohio. "Lordy, I hope she comes from up there, but I don't think I had better inquire too closely into her past," I said to myself as I went smiling away into the soft smoky night.

# NOTES OUT OF A MAN'S LIFE

# NOTES OUT OF A MAN'S LIFE [1]

## NOTE 6



I MAKE notes only of fragmentary things. In one moment a dozen moods may pass through me.

I arise from sleep and am shaving in the bathroom. With each stroke of the razor my mood may change.

People come into the house—my secretary—the negro servant who will get my breakfast.

My wife walks along a hallway, my son sings in his room.

A house is a shut-in place into which many people bring their moods. What has happened to the secretary before she came—to the cook?

What is in my wife's mind, my son's mind?

People are trained to say certain formal words—"Good morning"—What do the words mean?

My secretary is making fair copy of a novel I have written. It is inadequate. A novel should be written that will comprehend all lives.

When I am at all sensitive to life the moods

[1] New Orleans, 1925.

of people beat upon me as waves beat upon a swimmer in the sea. I try to keep myself clear, but cannot.

I float in many lives, am distressed, made gay, made happy—a thousand times each day.

What I have learned, a little, is not to try to express in words my understanding of moods I feel in others. People prefer such things kept secret.

The cook, a splendid brown girl with a strong body, has quarreled with her brown man. He got drunk and took money from her. The story is all told by the way she walks into a room. I keep silent, watching. After a time, if I am lucky, if my day is to be a fortunate one for me, I will escape into one life, one impulse, and get it working down through my fingers. To do that both exhausts and relieves me.

However I leave a trail behind. This man or woman I might have loved. There was a marvelous tale I might have told.

"*Before my pen has gleaned my teeming brain.*"

Presently I shall die with a thousand, a hundred thousand tales untold. People I might have loved I shall not love.

As I stand in the bathroom preparing my body to receive others I am also preparing my mind. I came out of sleep a scattered thing, a sensitive plate ready to receive any sort of impression.



If my day is not to be a failure I must gather myself together and concentrate on one impression.

## NOTE 7

Nights come when the whole world seems more alive than during the day. Often I go tramping in empty streets on such nights, myself more alive than in the day. Others more alive too. Something electric is in the air, something everyone feels.

As E sat reading a book daylight came. She looked down the narrow street. Two young men, walking in the roadway, came to a street intersection. Their figures were but dimly seen. They stopped and seemed to kiss. When E told me of it she spoke of how the book she had been reading at that strange hour had made all the world seem strange. Then the embrace of the young men in the dawn. She had to struggle for a moment to get back again into reality.

## NOTE 8

I like my friend X. He is somewhat pompous and slow and is rather fat. Once or twice a year he comes to see me or I go to him.

He spends hours talking, telling over and over the most trite things. Then of a sudden he makes the most penetrating observations.

He was educated carefully and pronounces his words in the English manner.

When he was a young man an odd thing happened to him. He went to walk with a young lady on a Sunday afternoon. Some boys had built a house in a tree. There was a ladder going up. On a dare X and the young lady crawled up the ladder.

It was nice up there. The house had been built from a huge store box. They could just squeeze in.

They sat on a bench the boys had built in the box-house and forgot the passing of time. A great wind came up and blew the ladder away.

My friend was preparing for the church. The young lady was a virgin. They were in a wood a half hour's walk from town. It began to rain. They stayed in the tree all night.

Later X thought he might have managed to crawl down out of the tree but the young lady would not let him. She said she was afraid to be alone. When searchers came looking for them she would not let him cry out. She said it would cause a scandal, they would be laughed at.

She herself started a conversation about what people would think. She cried a good deal so he took her into his arms. He kissed her. Nothing else happened. There was no room.

However, as he always very carefully explained, nothing would have happened anyway.

Later he married her. Their life has always been that way. When she wants anything she cries.

As often happens with such couples there were children—four of them. He has educated them very carefully. They all bully him. When they want anything they cry or make a fuss and he surrenders.

He knows exactly what he is doing. He laughs at himself. Sometimes when he comes to see me he tells me the whole story. He has worked like a devil all his days, making money.

What he wanted was to be a scholar. Show him a priest in a long smock reading a book and he almost weeps.

"I would have been such a success, so cynical, so well behaved. A fat priest is something charming but look at me. I have missed my chance because I am tender-hearted," he says and laughs.

## NOTE 9

As to this matter of a man's relations to other men and to women. Directly—being a man—I have no relation to anything. I play—am of no direct importance. It may be that I sometimes fertilize another man or woman, mentally or physically. That seems to me quite accidental. If the thing were not done by me someone else might do it.

The woman who has a child, carrying it in her body, thrusting it forth in pain, can well feeling a direct relation between herself and trees, grasses, animals. I am much less the animal, being male. Often I pitch off into the world of fancy, losing, for the time being, all direct connection with the physical world.

I visit China, the South Seas, the frozen North. I talk to men, make love to women, play with children. I am, in fancy and during one day, a dozen other men. I live inside them, pick up objects with their fingers, think their thoughts, feel what they feel.

If I could stay quite completely in the world of fancy or in the physical world I might be satisfied. I stay in neither.

I am a candle blown by the wind. Soon I shall go out.

I go to the river where men are loading ships. I sit watching two strong negroes who are putting great timbers into the hold of a ship. What they touch with their great black fingers is something definite. I am envious of them.

In fancy I can build a whole city of beautiful houses. I can sail a ship on stormy seas, can lift great stones—but my fancies, that can come so swiftly and quickly, are as quickly blown away.

I sleep in a room in the midst of books. I write books. In one night, when I am sleepless, enough fancies come to me to make a whole library of books.

They come and go. Nothing stays. I produce nothing of any permanence. Men like me, feeling keenly this impermanence, have invented heaven and hell. "Better roast forever in hell than to disappear like a candle blown out," they say.

But the vision of heaven and hell is also a fancy.

The negro working on the docks is envious of me sitting and thinking. I am envious of him rolling the great timbers. He thinks me an aristocrat and I think him an aristocrat.

What would I not give to accomplish something definite—related to trees, the earth, the sky, the seas!

What would I not give to be a man, not the shadow of a man!

## NOTE 10

In New Orleans men in white clothes and women in light summer dresses are coming from the Cathedral. It is a hot still summer morning.

NOTES OUT OF A MAN'S LIFE.

My own figure, clad in white, pleases me as I come into the room.

On Sunday every negro, in town or in the country, who can raise the money, goes for a ride. They ride up and down on boats, on railroad trains, mules or street cars. If you have an automobile that will go but ten more miles sell it to a negro. He will take his wife and children, invite his friends. They will ride the ten miles joyfully and walk patiently back.

The negro woman who had washed my clothes white came in white to get my breakfast. Her voice is smooth, her body strong.

By washing my clothes she has made herself a part of me. I shall now eat the food cooked by her brown hands. The food will make white flesh on my bones.

For whole days I try being a black man. I sat once all night at a boat landing at Baton Rouge. It was hot and still. Mother Mississippi made a soft whispering little sound as her lips touched the land. The steamer had but one eye—a glowing headlight that shot up along the landing stage to a warehouse on a high bluff.

Soft swaying bodies, dancing, dancing, dancing. In the night the great bugs, that come out of the darkness to the light, also danced about the heads of the negro stevedores.

For a long time all was still. The negroes

came out of darkness into the light and the great bugs flew about their heads striking black faces but the negroes did not mind. Grain was being unloaded—thousands of sacks.

There was nothing for the white captain and the mate to do. The negroes had fallen into their rhythm. No good swearing now, shouting commands. The night was very hot.

I lay on my back in dusty weeds. Shuffle, shuffle—shuffle along.

Sadness too. The long reach of the silent empty river—the dead river that was once alive.

Ghostly echoes of cries, oaths. Explorers on the river, De Soto, La Salle, Tonti of the Iron Hand, keel-boat men, longhorn men, pilots on steamers, Mark Twain, "no bottom, no bottom, no bottom."

Human cries across nights, Mason, Big Harpe, Little Harpe, gamblers, steamboat men.

The Natchez—the Robert E. Lee.

Too late. Too late.

For myself I could have done without many things, Woolworth Buildings, the Henry Fords, the aeroplane, the automobile, modern Chicago, Detroit, the movies, the radio, Los Angeles, Miami.

I lay in the weeds by the big river all night, a thousand miles of empty river, no sound—the soft lap of little waves in soft mud, the shuffle of negro feet.

Hours passed—no song. It was midnight. On the deck of the boat the mate sat under a light reading a newspaper.

Then it began. Generations of load bearers in the bodies of these men, the blacks. Did something whisper to them out of the silent river?

First the soft beginning of laughter—out of the bowels of the ship. The laughter ran up the gangplank.

A cry. Oh, ah ho, ah ho, ah ho. Las' sack now. Soon de las' sack. Oh, ah ha, ah ha.

A dance in the bodies now. Swaying bodies going empty handed, dancing down a gangplank. (If you ever have to go all night down a steep hill try that step. See how easy it is. See how it rests the body.)

Dance going down-hill, rest that way, dance then coming up with two hundred pounds on your shoulders.

Keep dancing, rest dancing.

De las' sack, de las' sack.

On Sunday go ride in the white man's engine. Rest riding.

But keep the song, black man, don't lose the song.

When you lose that, we've got you, we whites.

We'll get you in the end, of course.

That's what makes the song sweet to hear while it lasts.

Will love of words be lost? Success, standardization, big editions, money rolling in.

When you get money you are respectable.

What has respectability to do with loving words? What words do you love? Who has passed on them? What authority has said they are respectable?

Words for every act of the body, for dark and gay thoughts.

The little singing sound made by a pen on paper. The tale whispered in the night and then forgotten.

Words going the way of the blacks, of song and dance.

Can you imagine sweet words in a factory, sing them, dance them?

In the end they will make factory hands of us writers too.

The whites will get us. They win.

Don't turn your back on the modern world. Sing that too, if you can, while the sweet words last.

# NOTES ON STANDARDIZATION

## NOTES ON STANDARDIZATION [1]

NOTES ON STANDARDIZATION.

THERE has been, for a long time now, and with America and Germany as the most outstanding leaders of the movement, a tremendous standardization of life going on in every country of the western world.

As an example of what I am trying to get at, let me start by restating a fact, well known to every American past forty, the obvious fact that within our own day there has come a great change in the mechanics of the everyday life of every American man, woman and child.

There have been these two things—the speeding up and the standardization of life and thought, the one impulse no doubt the result of the other.

In my own father's day, for example, there was not a man of our Ohio town, counting himself at all a person of intelligence, who did not know the name of the editor of every outstanding New York, Chicago, Cincinnati or New

[1] New Orleans, 1921. Taken from an article published in the *Double Dealer.*

Orleans newspaper. Not only the names but the personalities and dominant characteristics of many of these editors were known to men within the radius of the territories in which their newspaper circulated, and often far outside. The entire daily press of the country was dominated by men of strong individuality who were continually making a direct and powerful appeal out of their own complex minds to readers all over the country.

You have but to compare the city newspaper of today with that of a generation ago to get a quite startling realization of what has happened. In the newspaper world now are there any such towering figures as our fathers knew? If there are, who are they?

When it comes to that, does the average citizen of any American city today know or care who is editor of the newspaper he reads in the morning? A man doesn't think of personalities in connection with newspapers any more. The passing from active service of Colonel Henry Watterson, of the Louisville *Courier-Journal*, saw pass also the last of the old type of unique individuals impressing their personalities on people in general through the ownership or editorship of newspapers. Chicago, a city of the gods know how many hundred thousands nameless human beings drifting daily through crowded, noise-haunted streets, in and out of the doors of apartment and office buildings, department stores and factories, has two morning newspapers, printed in English.



Paris, a city half the size of Chicago, has some thirty French daily newpapers.

And Paris, you will remember, is inhabited by one people while Chicago has within its limits a conglomeration of peoples from all over the world, newly come together and trying to make of themselves one people—a new people—the Americans of the future.

There is something very amazing indicated by all this.

In one city the attempt is being made to channel the minds of all men into one iron groove while in the other the idiosyncrasies of individuals and groups are given breathing space and many channels of expression. The impulse has its roots in the somewhat strange notion, that has for a long time been becoming more and more prevalent among us, a notion that to conform to type is man's highest mission.

A rather strange doctrine, that, to be so universally accepted in "the land of the free and the home of the brave?"

It was I believe a doctrine held in high esteem in Germany in the days of the Hohenzollerns. There they succeeded in making the doctrine the national ideal. They made every man a soldier, disciplined every citizen with an iron hand, crushed the individuality out of every-one and succeeded finally in creating the terrible military machine that made the rest of the world tremble in anticipation of the time when it would be set going against them but that, by an ironic turn of fate, the French, perhaps the most individualistic people in the world, did manage to turn aside at the Marne.

What I have said about the newspaper field is equally true of the general magazine field and it is pretty much true nowadays of the whole book-publishing business.

In the beginning the publication of magazines and books in America was almost entirely a cultural undertaking, with thoughts of profit taken into consideration only as a secondary element. Nowadays single organizations own, edit and publish sometimes as many as a dozen magazines. These magazines are run through the shops in bunches, as the modern factory turns out cheap furniture. I beg of you, if you are under the illusion that there is left any individuality among them, go to the nearest news stand and run your eye over the covers of a dozen popular magazines.

On the cover of each magazine is to be seen the same Broadway conception of womanly beauty. She has tilted her head a little more or less to this or that side. Now she is swinging a golf stick, now driving an automobile. Oh, ho, it is winter. She is now setting forth for the frozen lake clad in expensive furs and with a pair of skates on her shoulder.

There is one thing for which I have always been devoutly thankful. I have never seen this magazine cover female in the flesh and I hope I never shall. I try to be a gentleman and would dislike being caught in the act of throwing a brick at the head of a lady.

As for the contents of these magazines some of them have been able to develop a type of writer who is really quite amazingly clever.

When you bear in mind that all of these magazines are run primarily for the purpose of the advertising pages and that the first thing always to be borne in mind by the editors is the building up and holding of tremendous circulations, it will be easily understood why America had to develop a special type of writer to meet the demand.

A sort of continual and terrible perversion of life goes on. After all there are human men and women in America. Where among us live these creatures of the popular magazine short story, the best-selling novel or the moving picture? You read the stories published in these magazines and they are very skilfully done. There is a strange exterior semblance of life in the people who parade before us and do for our edification these brave clever or humorous stunts.

The trick when analyzed is very simple. The appearance of life is given by exterior means entirely. The doctor's office, the city street, the vacant lot beside the factory, are described with an amazing finality and fulsomeness of detail. Into these places people are cast, wearing ordinary clothes such as a man is accustomed to see wrapped about the bodies of his friends and neighbors.

There is a kind of legerdemain that with practice may be acquired. Having tricked your reader by these purely mechanical details into having faith in the people you are writing about, you simply make these people do and say things no human being has ever really been known to do or say.

In the pages of these magazines no one ever acts as people do in life or thinks as people do in life and of course the writers of the stories care nothing for human life. To begin caring for human life, thinking of human life and trying to understand it a little, would so quickly destroy their technique, stop incomes and jerk the writers down off the pasteboard thrones.

The point is that such writers are, one and all, men who might have been at least half artists under decent conditions. They have been twisted out of their natural function as artists.

A magazine having a circulation of a million is in a rather ticklish position when it comes to handling any such matter as honest reactions to life. There are so many things the editors of all such magazines have to be careful about. All such basic human attributes as sex hungers, greed and the sometimes twisted and strangely perverted desires for beauty in human beings have to be let alone. The basic stuff of human life that all real artists, working in the medium of prose, have handled all through the history of writing has to be thrown aside. The writer is perpetually called upon to seem to be doing something while doing nothing at all. There is the perpetual tragedy of unfulfilment.

Every intelligent man knows that, since Eve tempted Adam with the apple, no such thing as a pure man or woman has ever existed in the world but these poor devils are compelled to believe, against all the dictates of their common sense, that purity is a kind of universal human attribute and departure from it a freakish performance. In order that none of the million subscribers be lost or any good advertiser offended they are forced to spend their lives firing off blank cartridges or shooting pith-balls at pig bladder.

I remember that my father, a man given to outbursts of picturesque cursing, used to sometimes startle us children by some such pronouncement as this (some neighbor had perhaps won his disfavor): "Damn his hide. I hope he has to live all the rest of his days in a pie factory with a muzzle on," he cried, shaking his fist at the neighbor's house.

. . . . . . .

The man in the street, engaged in the important matter of watching the baseball score, or wondering how he can beat the income tax or the races, will also be wondering what all this has to do with human life in America.

It has a good deal to do with it I should say.

When one thinks of America as it was, but a few generations ago, a vast wilderness across which railroads had to be laid, whose forests had to be cut away and whose cities were yet to be built, one can understand that there was a time in America when to be perpetually on the go, to be a hustler and a go-getter, was a kind of moral duty.

Then perhaps there was no time to be wasted in this foolishness of trying to understand each other, of trying to really call up before ourselves, through the work of our artists, something of the inner quality of lives. To be a go-getter was then perhaps a moral duty. A tree might have fallen on the head of the pioneer who for a moment lost himself in the effort to understand his neighbor. Alertness was the mood of the times.

It may be now that a time has come to ask ourselves questions.

Are our lives worth living?

Is it living at all to spend all of our best years in helping to build cities larger, increase the number and size of our factories, build up individual fortunes, make more dirt and noise and indulge in an ever-increasingly louder talk of progress?

Or is there a quieter, more leisurely and altogether more charming way of life we might begin to live, here in America, instead of having to run off to Europe to find it?

Whether the time has come to ask the question or not, it is being asked. That is the most important question the younger generation is asking. A sharp and ever more and more searching criticism of all the old American shibboleths is going on. Books are being written and printed today that simply could not have found a publisher five or ten years ago and a new and vastly more intelligent audience has already been developed for these books. In the future—sometime perhaps—we will have less loud talk of freedom and a more determined individual effort to find freedom for expression of lives.

When it comes to the Arts it is probably true that there is today more vitality expressed in America in sculpture, painting and writing, than in any of the older cultural centers of Europe.

The simple fact of the matter is that, if America will but begin to turn more of its natural vitality into the Arts, and if we begin to think more of quality than of quantity and more of living than of accumulating, and also if we can bear, without too much flinching, a determined criticism, I myself believe—and I am far from alone in this belief—that the center of culture for the whole western world may be shifted to America. In short America may become the center for a new channeling of life through the Arts, for a new renaissance.

In this article I have used the word "culture" several times, perhaps too often. It is a rather dangerous word to use to Americans and frightens some of us horribly. As a people we have always been most fearfully afraid of being called cultural. The idea has become mixed up in our heads with the study of geometry, the translation of Homer in schools, and such things. Not fancying these things we have become almighty proud of our low-browishness. There is however no necessity of our being too proud of our lack of subtlety in definitions.

# ALFRED STIEGLITZ

# ALFRED STIEGLITZ[1]

*Old man—perpetually young—we salute you.*
*Young man—who will not grow old—we salute you.*



I do not know, cannot know, when the thing happened to Alfred Stieglitz that made him a man beloved of many men. It may have been when he was a young fellow but, as he is an American, it perhaps did not happen with him—within him—until he had come into middle life. In any event any man going into the presence of Alfred Stieglitz knows that, on a day long ago, something did happen that has sweetened the man's nature, made him a lover of life and a lover of men. It has come about that many men go gladly and freely in and out of this man's presence. Knowing the man you may not agree with his judgments on this or that piece of work, you may say to yourself that he talks too much, is too much and sometimes too consciously the prophet of the new age, but in a moment, and after you have gone out of his physical presence, something happens within you too.

[1] Written in 1919. Published in *The New Republic.*

You are walking in a city street and suddenly you walk more gladly and lightly. Weariness goes out of you. You are in a street lined with buildings, for the most part ugly and meaningless, but something within is now telling you that a breath can blow even this colossal stone and brick ugliness away. Again, and now quite definitely and permanently, you know that although men have blundered terribly in building up the physical world about themselves and although most men have been incurably poisoned by the ugliness created by men there is at the very heart of humanity a something sweet and sound that has always found and always will find among men, here and there, an individual to strive all his life to give voice to man's inner sweetness and health.

As for myself, I have quite definitely come to the conclusion that there is in the world a thing one thinks of as maleness that is represented by such men as Alfred Stieglitz. It has something to do with the craftsman's love of his tools and his materials. In an age when practically all men have turned from that old male love of good work well done and have vainly hoped that beauty might be brought into the world wholesale, as Mr. Ford manufactures automobiles, there has always been, here in America, this one man who believed in no such nonsense, who perhaps often stood utterly alone, without fellows, fighting man's old fight for man's old inheritance—the right to his tools, his materials, and the right to make what is sound and sweet in himself articulate through his handling of tools and materials.

There is something definite to be said in this matter, something very important to be said. Whether or not I am clear-headed enough to say it I can't be sure. What I do know is that in some way the figure of Alfred Stieglitz stands at the heart of the matter. What I think, I believe, is that we Americans, in the age that has just passed, have been a very sick people. Let me speak of that for a moment. To me it seems that the outward signs of that impotence that is the natural result of long illness are all about us in America. It is to be seen in our architecture, in the cowboy plays in our moving picture theaters and in our childish liking of the type of statesman who boasts of walking softly and carrying a big stick. True maleness does not boast of its maleness. Only truly strong men can be gentle tender patient and kindly; and sentimental male strutting is perhaps always but an outpouring of poison from the bodies of impotent men. Might it not be that with the coming into general use of machinery men did lose the grip of what is perhaps the most truly important of man's functions in life —the right every man has always before held dearest of all his human possessions, the right in short to stand alone in the presence of his tools and his materials and with those tools and materials to attempt to twist, to bend, to form something that will be the expression of his inner hunger for the truth that is his own and that is beauty. A year ago Mr. Gilbert Cannan made this dark and threatening comment on our modern life. "Befoul the workman's tools and materials long enough," said Mr. Cannan, "and in the end the workman will turn on you and kill you."

I myself think we have gone rather far on the road of befouling. To me it seems that the Ford automobile is about the final and absolute expression of our mechanical age—and is not the Ford car an ugly and ill-smelling thing? And against the Ford car and the vast Ford factories out in Detroit I would like to put for a moment the figure of Alfred Stieglitz as the craftsman of genius, in short the artist. Born into a mechanical age and having lived in an age when practically all American men followed the false gods of cheapness and expediency, he has kept the faith. To me his life is a promise that the craftsmen, who are surely to be reborn into the world, will not have to kill in order to come back into their old inheritance. Against the day of their coming again Alfred Stieglitz has held to the old faith with an iron grip. Through perhaps almost the single strength of this man, something has been kept alive here in America that we had all come near to forgetting.

I have been walking in the streets of New York and thinking of my friend Alfred Stieglitz and suddenly he no longer stands alone. Certain other figures appear and in them I understand in him certain impulses I have not always understood. I have myself come into the years of manhood in an age of Ford factories, and often enough I have run with the pack. Too often in my own work I have not been patient enough. I have stopped half way, have not gone all the way. Shame comes to me and suddenly memories appear. I remember that when I was a lad in Ohio there were in my town certain fine old workmen come down into our new age out of an older time. In fancy now I see again two such men and hear them speaking of their work as they stand idling in the evening before one of the stores of my town. The lad, who was myself, is fascinated by their talk and stands behind them, listening. And now suddenly one of the workmen has remembered something he wants to explain to his fellow. They are both wagonmakers and each, in his young manhood, has served his long years of apprenticeship and has gone on his workman's journey. The workman who is talking is trying to explain to his fellow how, in a certain shop where he once worked in the state of Vermont, they made a wagon felloe.

"You come on," he says, and the two old men go away together along the street in the dusk of a summer evening with a boy tagging at their heels. How sharply their figures remain in my mind, the two old lovers filled with a man's love, we moderns have almost forgotten. And now they have gone to one of the two wagon shops in the town and one of them has lighted a lamp and has opened his chest of tools. How affectionately he handles them and how bright and clean and sharp the tools are. He begins fitting two pieces of wood together. "At that place I was telling you about we did it like this. Afterward I found out a quicker way but I believe the harder way is the best. It makes a better joint, stands up better in all kinds of weather; that's what I mean," the old workman says—and how sharply his figure comes back to me now as I think of Alfred Stieglitz, the prophet of the old workmen who by the intensity of his love of tools and materials has made himself such an outstanding American artist.

There is another man in my mind of the Stieglitz sort. He lives now at Cleveland, Ohio, where he runs a book store, but some twenty years ago he came to America from Germany as a workman, as a church organ builder. On an evening last summer he walked and talked with me and as he walked and talked his mind went back to his boyhood in a German town. He spoke of the workmen in his father's shop and their treatment of him when he was a lad, learning his trade. When he had grown careless the workman, whose assistant he was, did not report the matter to the superintendent but took the blame on himself. Then the old workman and the boy looked into each others' eyes. "I didn't cut up any more monkey-shines after that," said the bookseller of Cleveland.

On Sundays, when he was a lad, my friend at Cleveland walked in the state forest with his father. Other workmen also came with their sons. One of them went to touch one of the trees with his fingers. Soon now that particular tree would be offered for sale and already the workman had put his hand on his materials. He intended to be on hand and to be a bidder when that particular tree was offered for sale. "After my father died," my friend at Cleveland said, "I went to a sale in the forest and bought a tree just because I had once seen my father look long and hungrily at it and because I knew he would want me to get my hands on it and work it up."

And this man of Cleveland came to America to be a foreman in one of our church organ factories. He didn't last long. He quit because they used nails instead of wooden pegs in the factory where he was employed. The owner of the factory tried to reason with him but he quit. "Here you have to do things in a hurry, in the American way. What's the difference? No one knows. They can't tell the difference."

But my friend quit. The fact that nails were used instead of wooden pegs seemed to him a quite sufficient explanation of his inability to stay. He thought the nails affected, in a quite poisonous way, the tone of the instruments. He seemed to care about that. "Every time I drove one of the nails it hurt my arm," he said, and there was something that hurt him too when he heard the other workmen driving the nails. The sound hurt him. He winced when he spoke of it and quite suddenly one saw that the sound of the nails being driven into the materials he loved was to him what the sound of the nails being driven into the cross of Christ might have meant in the ears of a primitive Christian.

It is just the spirit of these men that has always been alive and has always been kept alive in the person of Alfred Stieglitz, the photographer. In a peculiar way he has made himself an outstanding figure in the lives of innumerable American artists. In the beginning of this article I said that something must have happened to him long ago. He saw something we others haven't often seen. To me and to many other men I know his figure has been sharply de-

fined, and as the years pass is becoming more 
and more sharply defined, as the type of the old workman whose love of his tools and his materials has been so passionate that he has emerged out of the workman to become the artist.

And perhaps that he is a photographer is significant too. It may well be the most significant thing of all. For has he not fought all of his life to make machinery the tool and not the master of man? Surely Alfred Stieglitz has seen a vision we may all some day see more and more clearly because of the fight he has made.

# NOTES OUT OF A MAN'S LIFE

# NOTES OUT OF A MAN'S LIFE [1]

## NOTE 11

NEW ORLEANS will some day be again one of the greatest American cities, perhaps as great as New York. Goods run down-hill from the whole Mississippi Valley to New Orleans. It is a great funnel. Down the long watery groove made by the Mississippi the goods slip into the hold of ships. To the east and west of the great Valley all goods must be lifted over mountains.

NOTES OUT OF A MAN'S LIFE.

The railroads killed the river. Now the automobile, the aeroplane and the river may crush the power of the railroads. The aeroplane will take care of passengers for long hauls, the automobiles and trucks will handle local traffic, heavy slow-moving freights will again take to the river.

Coal for export, iron, corn, wheat, cotton. Incoming freights—coffee, sugar, hemp—in time lumber—will go up river.

The Mississippi will live again but men will still hunger for the old days.

[1] New Orleans, 1925.

For song mostly. The negroes are giving up singing. In the old days all negro laborers sang. Now they only sing in the back country where the modern age with its perverted hunger for an efficiency that is not efficient has not yet penetrated.

## NOTE 12

I awake. I am depressed. My nerves have gone back on me. I sleep in the room where I work, liking to be near books, my desk, the smell of ink.

When I awake I know I cannot work but I arise hopefully. There is a pile of white sheets that I have covered so that dust does not settle on them.

Now I brush the cloth of my desk, rearrange my books and papers.

I shall not write today. My nerves are on edge. I am incapable of sustained thought or feeling. I think perhaps I am getting old, that my capacity for sustained work is gone forever. The thought sends a shudder through my frame. I shall walk about today seeing strong well men everywhere. I want to kill some man, take from him his youth and strength and go gayly on my way.

There is a strong man who thinks he wants fame. He would give anything for fame. Well

I have had a little of that. He may have mine. Let's trade.

I want only strength to sit here at my desk all day. I want the words and sentences to march across the sheets. Let someone else sign all I do. If any fame is to come to me let someone else have it.

I want to work. It is my life. I want to gather together the thousand impressions of life that have come to me.

I want to put meaning and music into prose.

But I shall not be able to work today. My nerves are shattered.

I must go out, flee from this desk, go walk in the streets.

I put on my clothes and go away. I feel like weeping when the day comes wherein I cannot work.

## NOTE 13

Popular fictionists are born, not made. You have to be that way. What is acquired is a stopping place. People want something finite, something definite. If there is a certain limitation to the searchings of your own mind you are all right.

You believe for example that if labor could come into power the world would be a better place to live in. The obvious fact that the average man of labor has in him a certain sweetness just because he is not in a position of power must be overlooked. You must get men and women as definite things, working within definite limits.

Most popular novelists have the newspaper headline point of view. Let a woman be murdered and she becomes automatically beautiful. The cowboy is brave, the thief bold and dangerous.

You work always within a limited circle.

The thing can't be done effectively unless you are born that way. Nothing is more pitiful than the sight of a man trying to be popular who is not born to it.

## NOTE 14

Since I have been a boy there has been one thing from which I have never been able to escape. Money—the desire for money—the need of money has always been hurtful to me and to all the men and women I have known.

Often I walk about looking at others. There is a rich man passes me on the street. I follow him to his house. He goes through a gate into a wide garden. Would I enjoy life in such a garden—in such a house?

Some men inherit money and it is handled for them by some agent. The agent however must needs be quick, alert, on guard.

I am always being caught off-guard. When I have accumulated a little money—a few thousand dollars—someone comes and takes it.

Then I am poor again and am worried. I cannot manage things, cannot get things clear. When I sit down to work there comes a man to collect a bill and I have no money to pay.

When I want peace I go among the poor. They are poor because they are not clever, cannot get the best of me or anyone.

It is because life is so difficult we come in the end to welcome death.

It is not only that others get the best of us about money but in turn we get the best of others. All are on guard.

When I have the best of another I feel cheaper than when he has the best of me.

## NOTE 15

I have a letter from a woman. I cannot answer it. She has written a book which I have read. She was born rich, never in her life earned money. When she had got to a certain age she began adventuring. At once she went to Europe and lived there most of her life. A business man in America must have handled her affairs.

When I saw the woman in the flesh we had something for each other. Perhaps she felt in me something of the soil. I remember one evening sitting in a room with her. I felt her, as I might have felt some warm exotic plant.

When she wrote books however all became lost. The people of her books moved about like things in the air. No one in her books had any roots in the soil. I do not like ugliness but to me the soil, the houses in which poor people live, the overalls of workers, the brown strong gnarled hands of workers are not ugly.

Often these things have for me a strange haunting and unforgettable beauty that cannot be matched in the most delicate fabrics, in the most elegant houses.

## NOTE 16

I do not think of God. I think of the things outside my window—the life on sidewalks, in buildings. Everything changes. Soon there will be a new scene and I will not be sitting here writing. Shortly thereafter the last faint fragrance of me will have been blown away.

That is rather wonderful. If any fragrance of me remained there would be a stench too. I have not achieved clearness often. In my work I have seldom come quite clear.

# WHEN THE WRITER TALKS

# WHEN THE WRITER TALKS [1]

WHEN THE WRITER TALKS.

SUCH a strange place to be in. I am in a huge western State university. It is night. I have been lecturing on Modern American Writing before a thousand young men and women. What an absurd thing to try to do. There I have been standing, before all these young men and women, talking and talking. How silly! I did it for money. I have been broke and have been lecturing to get some money into my pockets. I would like so well the things money buys—cigarettes, horses, warm clothes, a fine house to live in. I would so like to have a great deal of money. Why does not someone who has ten or fifteen million dollars give me a million, or a half million, anyway? If you meet a man bothered by his money tell him about me. I would like to wear clothes made of delicate fabrics, gay, brightly-colored neckties, flashing vests, plaid socks. I would like a string of race horses, a farm, a yacht. There is in me something that likes to strut before men, make a splash of color in the street where I walk. I do not want the women to wear all of the bright

[1] Published in *The Literary Review,* 1925.

gay things. The little city girl, who works in a factory or in an office and spends all of her money to buy clothing she can ill afford, has won my heart. She is my sister. Long ago, in some old European corner, she and I belonged to the same tribe.

And so I am lecturing to get money to buy the necessities of life and a few gay things, not necessary, for myself, for my wife, for my sons.

But what an odd experience, this lecturing. There are a thousand young men and women in the hall where I have been speaking. What do they think of me, standing up there and trying to say bright wise things to them? As I talked I had an idea. I shall propose it to my lecture manager. It is inconceivable to me that anyone should want to come to hear any man lecture. Perhaps students are bullied into it. Husbands are brought by wives who are after culture and who have the erroneous notion that I am cultured. I shall propose to my manager a scheme. People may hear me lecture for 25 cents but shall be charged $1 for the privilege of staying away. Millions will want to stay away. We shall both grow rich like a prize fighter and his manager. I have such brilliant business ideas.

The lecturing excites me. When I come out on the platform something happens. There is an actor sleeping in me and now he is awake. I stand, pause for effect, I become for the moment something I have never been before, walk in a new way, look at people out of new eyes. The world of the actor opens before me. What a strange world it is. Now this being, that is myself, is no longer myself. My body, my voice, my mind are instruments I have to learn to play. I do it badly enough.

I have lectured in the large hall and most of the people who have heard me have gone away. There are, however, twenty or thirty young men and women who have got me into a smaller room and are asking me questions.

Lord God of the mountains and valleys preserve me! Every question is so fundamental. These people now firing questions at me want to become writers in their turn. They are asking me how to do it and I am trying to answer. My bitterest enemy would be glad if he could see me now, if he knew how silly and helpless I feel inside myself. Had I never any modesty? What has become of it? I am actually trying to answer the questions. I think of Ben and Paul and Joe—wits all of them. In fancy I can see Ben giving an imitation of me as a lecturer. Thank Heavens, they are not here!

Why is money so hard to come by? There is so much of it about. If you see the man with the superfluous million do remember my name. It may be he is worried about his income tax. Tell him I shall not worry.

The young men and women are asking me questions that—if I could answer them at all—it would take a long book to answer. If I could answer them at all how wise I should be.

Everything that has to be so definitely said so falls to pieces when said. It becomes at once half a lie. There is a kind of insult in answering off-hand questions that apparently mean so much to the one who asks. If anyone actually took my answers seriously or remembered them it would be terrible.

. . . . . .

Poets I fancy come off better at this business. They go about reading their poetry. Poetry read, and when the poet has a good voice, is a way of singing. My father was once in the show business and did a song and dance. What rotten luck that I can neither sing nor dance.

I dare say actors come off all right. Someone else has written the lines they speak. An actor when he does not make a hit can always blame the play. Playwrights should never become actors and the actor should never write a line. The alibi is one of the prime necessities of life.

There is too much pretense in this standing up, as I am doing now, and pretending to think quickly and accurately before a lot of people. How do I know I can think at all—even in a quiet place and when I am alone? Why, I am a story-teller, not a thinker.

The questioners are very insistent. They keep at me. I fire off answers. Something inside me is beginning to grow tired. In a moment I shall fly off the handle. I will give smart impertinent answers perhaps to the most sensitive of all these people.

When I was myself a young writer I once began asking questions of another and older writer and he answered me rudely, with a vulgar fling of his hand, dismissing me. It was an experience I never forgot. The questions I had asked were of such deep importance to me—just at that time in my life.

I wanted to know how to have my cake and eat it, how to write just what I pleased and yet get well paid. You see what an important question that may be to a young writer but I cannot answer it. A whole lifetime has not taught me the answer.

That is only one of the questions now being flung at me. I feel like an animal pursued by enemies. Help, I am getting groggy. Why do so many people want to be writers anyway? There is a young man in the crowd who has just the look in his eye people always have when they are about to ask an impossible question. If he asks it I shall fling my watch at his head.

Someone rescues me. He is a professor in the

college and has perhaps seen the tired puzzled look in my eyes. Or perhaps he is one of the men responsible for getting me to make that particular speech and is afraid—as I am myself—that in another moment I shall betray my ignorance of all the so deadly important things I am supposed to know about and that I do not know.

I have escaped and am walking under the stars with the professor. When we are alone together we both become human. I look at him and he looks at me. We laugh a little. I have a hunch about him. It may be his hand, I suddenly see quite clearly as we walk under a street lamp, that betrays him. "Were you ever a farmer? Did you ever hold the handles of a plow?" I ask and it turns out that he was indeed once a young farmer in a county of Ohio where I also as a young man worked on a farm. "Perhaps we once plowed adjoining fields," I think but do not inquire too closely as I like the picture that now floats up into my mind. I fancy him plowing on a sloping hillside while on another hillside, across a valley, I am also plowing. It is spring. How sweeet the earth smells under our feet.

. . . . . .

And now I am at my hotel in the university town and have gone upstairs to my room. The other plowman is now lecturing every day in this university and I am going about delivering lectures about the art of writing.

"You cannot be a great man and be human. I would like to be a great man. I so detest men who think themselves important. It is so nice to be unknown, to slip quietly through streets, seeing life while remaining unseen, feeling life, yourself unseen and unknown." Dancing thoughts in my head now. Alone in my room I could make such a wonderful speech.

I am ashamed to light the light in my room at the hotel. Why am I not a praying man? It would be so helpful to pray, for wisdom let us say. "This lecturing business is so exciting and interesting. I love it.

"This lecturing business is so terrible. It makes me feel so cheap."

And now I have crawled into bed and my light is out for the night. Faces crowding up to me, lips ask questions. I float off to sleep accompanied by a sea of floating questioning faces.

But just before I sleep I think—there was that place in my lecture. By making it just a little different I shall get more of a rise out of my audiences.

It is the showman in me who comes back and who takes command just before I float off to sleep.

NOTES OUT OF A MAN'S LIFE

# NOTES OUT OF A MAN'S LIFE [1]

## NOTE 17

You lie in bed in the early morning half asleep, half awake. Someone is moving in the house. In the street outside feet are shuffling on the sidewalk.

Full consciousness is just before you and back of you lies the lack of consciousness, sleep and dreams. Chance may send you either road.

In such a state I invariably become something other than myself. This morning I became an old Frenchman living in the city of New Orleans. My wife was younger than myself. There was a flirtation going on between her and another Frenchman. The other Frenchman had long been my friend.

He came often to see me, wanting really to see my wife. To get him she would have to break down his loyalty to me.

For a long time the play went on. There was material for a complete novel as the swift scenes passed racing through the field of my fancy. Although I had become the old Frenchman, felt

[1] New Orleans, 1925.

all he felt, knew his thoughts, his feelings, he was also outside me and presented himself as a charming ridiculous old fellow.

## NOTE 18

I have often wondered at the relationship of people to the animal side of life.

Farmers, cattle-raisers, steamboat men, railroad men—know certain things about life, about animals, others do not know.

A poet I know was not well and went into the country to restore his health. As he was poor he had to work and so hired himself to a farmer. He was set to pitching manure.

Days and days of that. In time the green fields became to him but great heaps of manure. All became manure in the end.

The literature of the South is far removed from the soil. The stench is gone out of it. New Orleans, for example, is a city of smells. It reeks with smells from the earth, the sea, the river, the houses, the markets, the swamps. In the moist heavy air the smells hang all day and all night but in Southern stories nothing is mentioned but the magnolia.

As though in resentment at thus being singled out the magnolia will not be touched. It is a great white flower—splendid like a splendid woman—but touch it with but the tip of the finger or the nose and it becomes black. It also becomes manure.



## NOTE 19

The writer is seeking a certain tune, a rhythm. When he has caught it the words and sentences flow freely. There is a new cunning, a new majesty to his thoughts. To speak of him as working is absurd. As well speak of a stream working as it flows down to the sea.

Tales are everywhere. Every man, woman and child you meet on the street has a tale for you. In the old days in Chicago I used to come out of my room after writing for three or four hours and sometimes had to walk along looking down at the sidewalks.

When I had been working well there was a kind of insanity of consciousness. There may be little nerves in the body that, if we could bear having them become sensitive enough, would tell us everything about every person we meet.

I confess I am more sensitive to women than to men. If I had actually—with my body—made love to all the women toward whom I have felt love I would be dead long since.

For several years now I have been a semi-public character. My person, my morals, my character, my impulses as a writer have been discussed in public prints.

I have never thought any of the critics who have dissected me have got me right. Perhaps no man ever thinks another has got him right.

The point is that there is no use concealing anything. I am a sort of showman. If it were possible I would like to be a quiet retiring gentleman, concealing everything from my fellows.

There is no flavor to such nakedness. Nothing worthwhile knowing can be concealed. Telling what you already know is an insult to your intelligence.

And anyway, surfaces—houses in which people live, the clothes they wear—these things have their own value—their own possibilities of beauty.

In the streets of Chicago I walked with my eyes on the sidewalk refusing to look at people because their faces all had stories to tell and I could not receive them.

There was no strength in me to tell the tales. I bumped against people and several times came near being killed by motors.

I went to the lake. The lake, the sea, trees, rivers, negroes working in fields, these things rested me so that I could feel and work again.

When I was rested I went into a room where a woman sat. Let us suppose this to have happened when I was young. Her being married or not married had nothing to do with the matter.

She spoke of the theater, of the work of some painter—of music. If she were of an age that made her physically attractive to me two conversations went on. We spoke certain words and thought others. Often things hung in the balance. A word from her or from me would have opened up vast reservoirs of possibilities in our relations.



When I was younger, stronger, and perhaps more foolish, I used to think it would be well if everyone spoke their hidden thoughts aloud. Later I grew away from that notion. No one is good enough, strong enough, rich enough.

What I have just now been writing related to work, that is to say to writing, singing, dancing, painting, is difficult to say in words.

The relation you seek always exists. The rhythm you are seeking in any of the arts lies just below the surface of things in nature. To get below the surface, to get the lower rhythm into your hands, your body, your mind, is what you seek but having achieved it you are soon exhausted. It is necessary to come back to the surface, to be like a tree or a field. Men who can work at any time in any art have no relation to their art at all. Their relation to their work has no more reality than the giving of her body by a prostitute has to do with the reality of love.

## NOTE 20

NOTES OUT OF A MAN'S LIFE.

A woman reappears with whom I am presumed to have had an affair. In reality the affair did not come off but now she is quite convinced it did.

For some months—during a summer several years ago—the woman and I were much together. She was at a hotel in the mountains and I had gone to visit an acquaintance, a painter, in a nearby cabin.

The painter had been very lonely until I came and then, after I came, he suddenly began working.

That was all right for him but I could not work. I was in one of my dead indolent periods. His industry drove me mad. I could not bear the sight of him, working madly.

Like an idle woman I became a flirt to pass the time. I took up with the woman at the hotel who was glad enough to have me. She was one of the sort destined to play always along the dead line, never by any chance stepping over.

Well, I served her purpose, she mine. I walked with her in the fields, in the woods.

At night sometimes we came back to her hotel at two o'clock. All the other guests at the hotel gossiped. My friend, the painter, laughed. He was working. "Why do you not work? What are you up to? Such a woman—the devil."

He did not understand that I could not work. I was nasty inside, a mess.

So was the woman. We were fellows—for the time.

Her reputation was being ruined—or made. In reality she wanted the name of having affairs with men without having them. There are many such women.

One night—the moon was shining—it was midnight.

We sat down in the darkness by a little creek. In an open field nearby two little wild animals made love.

Afterward I thought we came near something but I was wrong. In the woman's fancy, later, that may have been the time and place when it happened.

Suddenly I was through with her. I left my friend and went away to the city. After another month I began working. Inside myself some minute readjustment had been made. I felt clean and healthy again.

I did not see the woman, did not think of her. My sudden disappearance had stirred up endless talk. I was heartless—had taken what I wanted and had gone away. The woman went about looking sad, a wronged woman. My friend, the painter, used to tell about it and laugh.

When two years later I saw her she took me aside, into the darkness, and talked to me. It was at a party at a friend's house. She talked of the danger she had been in. For a month she did not know. What a relief when she found nothing serious had happened.

"I would not have asked you to marry me. You are an artist. We women must lead our own lives, take our own chances."

The woman has a conviction. I have not disturbed it. Some of her friends, to whom she has talked, think she has been badly treated.

I shall do nothing to disturb her conviction. It may be that such fancied experiences with men are the only kind she will ever have.

## NOTE 21

A man came yesterday and told me a story of his first affair with a woman. How we got on the subject I can't remember. Men often drift to it unconsciously. All relations are difficult and puzzling.

The man talking to me was fifty and gray, a dignified looking man with a mustache. As he talked his voice was somewhat sad. No doubt he regretted the passing years.

When he was fifteen he was employed about the house of a storekeeper. The storekeeper was forty-five and had married a woman of twenty-five. Often the man went away, for three or four days at a time.

The young man worked about the stable and in the house. He slept on a cot in a little room downstairs while the merchant and his younger wife slept upstairs.

At that time, my visitor told me, he had no idea of anything happening. When a woman was married she was married. What was settled was settled. About young unmarried girls he had thoughts enough but older married women —well, he did not think of them at all.

He was half a servant in the house where he then lived but when the man of the house went away his position changed. He and the young woman began to play about. As he walked along a hallway she came creeping up behind. She pushed him and ran away laughing.

When the storekeeper was out of town they were one day washing windows. The woman put the water on the windows and washed them clean and the young man dried them with a cloth. She had put on old clothes and her dress was torn. Perhaps she had purposely torn it. He kept catching glimpses of her round breasts. She looked at him and laughed.

That night on his cot he could not sleep and she could not sleep in her room. He had left the door of his room partly open and she came down stairs and creeping to the door looked in. He pretended to sleep and then, when she had returned to her own room upstairs, he crept up and looked in at her.

He did it three times and she did it three times and then, when he was doing it the fourth time, she whispered to him from the dark room.

He went in to her and all was silent. The whole affair was carried on in darkness and silence. In the daytime, after that, she never spoke to him except about his work and whereas, in the past, she had been rather indulgent she now became severe.

He was sure that, in the daytime, she succeeded in quite convincing herself nothing had happened.

Once when she had been very severe and had rebuked him in the presence of her husband he flared up and left the place.

There was an odd moment, the man woman and boy standing facing each other. Later the boy hoped she had been hurt by his desertion. He could not tell. She stood stoutly by her guns, as though nothing had happened. In the darkness and silence she had been very tender with him. Now she was as hard as a stone.

At any rate, my visitor said, if there had ever been any suspicion, she must, by her brutality, have firmly established herself with her husband that day when he left.

## NOTE 22

I had put a fellow novelist into one of my books. In a certain situation he had failed to draw the line and I said so.

NOTES OUT OF A MAN'S LIFE.

He came to visit me. His personal life was also involved and difficult. When I saw the position into which he had got himself by failing to draw the line in life, as he had failed to draw it in the fanciful life of his books, I took out of my book the brutal note in the reference to him.

It is all very well to call a man names who can get even with you but it is dreadful when you know he can't.

# AN APOLOGY FOR CRUDITY

## AN APOLOGY FOR CRUDITY[1]

For a long time I have believed that crudity is an inevitable quality in the production of a really significant present-day American literature. How indeed is one to escape the obvious fact that there is as yet no native subtlety of thought or living among us? And if we are a crude and childlike people how can our literature hope to escape the influence of that fact? Why indeed should we want it to escape?

AN APOLOGY FOR CRUDITY.

If you are in doubt as to the crudity of thought in America, try an experiment. Come out of your offices, where you sit writing and thinking, and try living with us. Get on a train at Pittsburgh and go west to the mountains of Colorado. Stop for a time in our towns and cities. Stay for a week in some Iowa corn-shipping town and for another week in one of the Chicago clubs. As you loiter about read our newspapers and listen to our conversations, remembering, if you will, that as you see us in the towns and cities, so we are. We are not subtle enough to conceal ourselves and he who runs with open eyes through the Mississippi

[1] From *The Old Dial,* 1916.

AN APOLOGY FOR CRUDITY.

Valley may read the story of the Mississippi Valley.

It is a remarkable story and we have not yet begun to tell the half of it. A little, I think, I know why. It is because we who write have drawn ourselves away. We have not had faith in our own people and in the story of our people. If we are crude and childlike that is our story and our writing men must learn to dare to come among us until they know the story. The telling of the story depends, I believe, upon their learning that lesson and accepting that burden.

To my room, which is on a street near the loop in the city of Chicago, come men who write. They talk and I talk. We are fools. We talk of writers of the old world and the beauty and subtlety of the work they do. Below us the roaring city lies like a great animal on the prairies, but we do not run out to the prairies. We stay in our rooms and talk.

And so, having listened to talk and having myself talked overmuch, I grow weary of talk and walk in the streets. As I walk alone an old truth comes home to me and I know that we shall never have an American literature until we return to faith in ourselves and to the facing of our own limitations. We must, in some way, become in ourselves more like our fellows, more simple and real.

For surely it does not follow that because we

Americans are a people without subtlety we are a dull or uninteresting people. Our literature is dull but we are not. Remember how Dostoievsky had faith in the simplicity of the Russians and what he achieved. He lived and he expressed the life of his time and people. The thing that he did brings hope of achievement for our men.

But we should first of all accept certain truths. Why should we Americans aspire to an appearance of subtlety that belongs not to us but to old lands and places? Why talk of intellectuality and of intellectual life when we have not accepted the life we have? There is death on that road and following it has brought death into much of American writing. Can you doubt what I say? Consider the smooth slickness of the average magazine story. There is often great subtlety of plot and phrase but there is no reality. Can such work be important? The answer is that the most popular magazine story or novel does not live in our minds for a month.

And what are we to do about it? To me it seems that as writers we shall have to throw ourselves with greater daring into life. We shall have to begin to write out of the people and not for the people. We shall have to find within ourselves a little of that courage. To continue along the road we are traveling is unthinkable. To draw ourselves apart, to live in little groups and console ourselves with the thought that we are achieving intellectuality is to get nowhere. By such a road we can hope only to go on producing a literature that has nothing to do with life as it is lived in these United States.

To be sure the doing of the thing I am talking about will not be easy. America is a land of objective writing and thinking. New paths will have to be made. The subjective impulse is almost unknown to us. Because it is close to life it works out into crude and broken forms. It leads along a road that such American masters of prose as James and Howells did not want to take but if we are to get anywhere we shall have to travel the road.

The road is rough. Who, knowing our America and understanding the life in our towns and cities, can close his eyes to the fact that life here is for the most part an ugly affair? As a people we have given ourselves to industrialism and industrialism is not lovely. If anyone can find beauty in an American factory town I wish he would show me the way. For myself I cannot find it. To me, and I am living in industrial life, the whole thing is as ugly as modern war. I have to accept that fact and I believe a great step forward will have been taken when it is more generally accepted.

But why, I am constantly asked, is crudity and ugliness necessary? Why cannot a man like Mr. Dreiser write in the spirit of the early Americans, why cannot he see fun in life? What we want is the note of health. In the work of Mark Twain there was something wholesome and sweet. Why cannot the modern man be also wholesome and sweet?

AN APOLOGY FOR CRUDITY.

To this I make answer that to me a man, say like Mr. Dreiser, is wholesome. He is true to something in the life about him and truth is always wholesome. Twain and Whitman wrote out of another age, out of an age and a land of forests and rivers. The dominant note of American life in their time was the noisy swaggering raftsman and the hairy-breasted woodsman. Today it is not so. The dominant note in American life today is the factory hand. When we have digested that fact, we can begin to approach the task of the present-day novelist with a new point of view.

It is, I believe, self-evident that the work of the novelist must always lie somewhat outside the field of philosophic thought. Your true novelist is a man gone a little mad with the life of his time. As he goes through life he lives, not in himself, but in many people. Through his brain march figures and groups of figures. Out of the many figures one emerges. If he be at all sensitive to the life about him and that life be crude the figure that emerges will be crude and will crudely express itself.

I do not know how far a man may go on the road of subjective writing. The matter, I admit, puzzles me. There is something approaching insanity in the very idea of sinking yourself too deeply into modern American industrial life.

But it is my contention that there is no other road. If a man would avoid neat slick writing he must at least attempt to be brother to his brothers and live as the men of his time live. He must share with them the crude expression of their lives. To our grandchildren the privilege of attempting to produce a school of American writing that has more delicacy and color may come as a matter of course. I hope that will be true but it is not true now. And that is why, with so many of the younger Americans, I put my faith in the modern literary adventurers. We shall, I am sure, have much crude blundering American writing before the gift of beauty and subtlety in prose shall honestly belong to us.

# KING COAL

## KING COAL [1]



At one time in my life I lived for nearly a year in mining towns, going from one of them to another and doing the work at which I then made my living and the experiences of that year did something to me, left on my sensibilities a kind of raw and tender place that has never quite healed. A great deal of water has run under my particular bridge since that year but sometimes yet I awake at night and find myself in imagination again on the main street of one of those towns and feel again, in the human beings about me, a kind of dreary horror of life unmatched anywhere except in the most dismal slum streets of our cities.

During the night it is true such towns, seen from some nearby hill, have a kind of magnificence. I walked from the hotel, through the main street, past stores, and in the old days past saloons. Nowadays I dare say the saloons have become bootlegging establishments with a frontage of bottles of grapejuice and Coca Cola and their proprietors are more prosperous.

Some ten or twelve years ago, however, they

[1] Written in New Orleans in the Winter, 1923. Published in *Forum*.

 were poor enough places. And over the goods on the shelves of the general store as over the faces of the idlers in the saloons and the sheets in the beds at your hotel lay a fine thin film of black dust. These millions of tons of black stones that burn, jerked so violently up out of the ground and hurled here and there in long trains over the country to distant towns and cities had not come out of ground without protest. They had at least left this ineffaceable trail of black dust behind. It was everywhere, on the little patches of grass that tried to struggle up out of the ground beside the miners' houses in the spring, on the leaves of the poor diseased-looking trees scattered about, in the little creases under the eyes of children, in the hems of the garments of the women, in the hair and beards of the men. The little nerves of the nostrils became coated so that there was an almost permanent dulling of the sense of smell and I constantly tasted coal dust in the food at the hotels.

When at night, however, I had walked through the town and had climbed by a winding earth road into the hills I looked back with a little gasp of astonishment that a thing seen near at hand could be so dismal and dreary and at a distance and at night so magnificent. Perhaps I am destined to get always, when I stand a little away and look at it, these two distinct impressions of every aspect of our industrial age. Always there is this feeling of the futility and the apparent meaninglessness of individual lives against this background of something huge, uncontrolled, and diabolically strong tramping over the land and leaving this black trail of dust behind.

I was in the hills above a mining town and it was night. In the darkness the sense of black dust lying over everything was lost. As I stood looking down the main street, the stores, with the dirty dust-covered windows, the miserable shed-like houses and the black-faced men tramping homeward through the streets, were lost to sight. Of the mining town in which these men and women were to live out whole lives there was nothing left but the street lamps that now looked like fireflies in the soft darkness below.

And the mines. The mines make themselves felt in the darkness. If the coal that came from the mines of the town above which I stood was coking coal there was also the long lines of coke ovens stretching away to the right and left and making each a soft glow of light in the darkness.

Noises arose. There was the rattling bang of a half carload of coal that went roaring down from the tipple. Engines were shunting coal cars about. They had a great rattling machine, larger than a miner's dwelling, that was bouncing and sorting the coal in a long shed perched high in the air above the mouth of the mine. I got sharply the sense of something huge breathing down there. The imagination leaped across the little space between sanity and insanity. At any rate the miner, the individual man or woman in the town below, became lost. He was now as indistinguishable as an ant, one of the swarm of ants that scurry away in all directions when you have kicked over an ant hill in the fields. Now and then a human could be seen in the distance. There was a glare of light from the headlight of a locomotive or from a torch burning beside the tracks and across the little patch of light the dark figure flitted.

There was no doubt something living there. Buried away under the ground men were boring and digging and blasting. There was even another railroad beneath the surface of the ground. In the darkness the rows of coke ovens were like the glistening teeth of a giant. Something sleeping in the ground under the hills was being troubled in its inner digestive parts and was ill. The giant was being made to spew forth coal that men in a million houses might be warmed on cold nights and that factories might be run both day and night in many towns and cities. As the Rotary Club member would say, "The old pep was being put into the modern industrial world." How sad that the process of doing it should involve all this dreariness, this thankless labor and this endless breathing, eating and wearing, like a veil over the garments, this film of black dust.



As for myself, I suppose there was something in me that perversely would not see splendor where splendor was so obviously intended. Since boyhood I had been told—first by my own father and by the older men of my home town in Ohio, the men who were interested in me and did want with all their hearts to set me going straight in life, and later by other men I met everywhere, in the cities and on trains and in the pages of magazines and newspapers and even by men of the colleges—that all of this roaring noise, this breathing of smoke and black dust, this quick throwing up and tearing down of cities, this thing we so grandiloquently call America's Industrial Progress, was a thing of meaning. Ye gods of darkness, get ye behind me. Give me eyes to see into the darkness at the foot of this hill. To me the whole thing has no meaning at all. I am unconvinced that mankind is going anywhere by this road. Show me wherein all this tickling of the lining of Earth's stomach until he becomes ill and spews forth these millions of tons of coal, wherein all this endless blackening of lives has brought anything at all of light beauty or meaning into the life of miner or mine owner, factory worker or stockholder in the shares of factories, and by my ungrown beard I swear I shall join the Elks, the Rotary Club and all the Progress Clubs that will have me and for the rest of my days shall write nothing but pep editorials for Chicago or Detroit newspapers.

Some evil fate it is that has made me so bad an American. I myself came from a town in Ohio that has not, at the time I write, become the stirring industrial center its Chamber of Commerce would like to make it. But all about it are towns that have been more successfully ambitious.

I have in mind now such a town. A few years ago it was an American village inhabited only by ex-farmers, by artisans, by a few professional men, doctors, lawyers and the like, and by the merchants. And what another thing altogether it has become now.

It happened that I saw life in the town in the days before the factories came and before mountains of coal lay heaped beside the railroad tracks.

The older life in such an American town of the Middle West was not, I suppose, ideal, but I have always had the feeling that something I very much value had begun to grow there before it became choked with coal dust. Mr. Van Wyck Brooks, Mr. Waldo Frank and others who have analyzed the influence of such towns have not told all the story. A little there was recognition of the rights of the individual to his idiosyncrasies. Queer Rabelaisian old fellows who knew how to laugh and how to arouse deep laughter in others abounded. In the stores and on the streets in the evening men talked of baseball, horseracing, the best and fastest way to husk corn and how was the best way to get along with a woman. And there were among us not a few men who had a love for books and learning.

In the town of which I am now speaking I remember there was an old man who had come there to rest from his adventures. Why he came I cannot say. He had been some sort of officeholder in the South during the reconstruction days after the Civil War and had perhaps made away with unlawful moneys which he thought had better be spent in an obscure place.

There was a good deal of rascality in him, let us say. Into his old eyes a wicked gleam came at times and I have walked with him and have seen how the figure of a handsome woman in the street made him strut like an old turkey cock, but he did love books and knew well his Shakespeare, his Burns, Milton, Goethe and Keats. To his house I went sometimes on sum-

KING COAL.

mer evenings with other fellows of the place, mere fledgling boys like myself, to sit on the front porch and to be his guest.

The house stood with its back to a small river that made a murmuring sound in the quiet evening and from the front porch we could look down, a half dozen blocks, into Main Street.

We gathered there on summer evenings to hear the old man spout poetry and we did not bring our "girls," the event being, we felt, a sort of "men only" affair.

The old man, who perhaps secretly regretted that he had not become a Keene or a Booth rather than a carpet-bagger, was given to moments of a sort of Rabelaisian broadness of development of the theme touched upon by the poet. He had little patches of white hair brushed forward from the back of his skull and as he walked up and down under a hanging lamp inside the house and behind a screen door he made a great business of running his hands through it.

I get inevitably a sharp contrast between these nights and later nights in the hills above mining towns and in the streets of roaring hustling industrial towns. For one thing there was leisure. The sleeping giant had not really been disturbed under the hills and had not yet set out upon his conquests.

And in the meantime, on the porch of the old

man's house, we lads sat mightily impressed by his learning and from inside the house came the cadence of the words of the poets.

KING COAL.

Before us lay the short residence street and at the end of that the main street. The Ford and the movies, products also of the Age of Progress, of the Age of Coal, had not yet come and automobiles of any sort were a rare sight.

We sat, you see, not thinking but having the songs of old singers poured into us. In all the houses along the streets lived people my companions knew. Even at that distance when a man or a woman went across the patch of light that marked the debouchment of the residence street into Main Street he was known to the young men sitting about me, by his gait, by the way he carried his shoulders or by a peculiar swing of the arms. There came a pause in the old man's proclaiming of the verses of the poets. I am somewhat loath to mention such details to sensitive readers but the truth is the old man was a great chewer of finecut tobacco and had a spittoon in the front room of his house beside the table on which his books lay.

"Well, now I am going to read you one of the greatest poems ever written in our language." He always said that no matter what poem he was about to read. He paused to put a fresh quid of tobacco into his mouth and to tuck it away out of the track of his tongue. Did not

KING COAL.

Demosthenes put little stones so when he spouted poetry by the seashore?

In any event there was a period of silence and at that moment a man passed through the spot of light at the end of the street. "There goes Ed Prousey. His daughter Emma has got into trouble. I bet you what, Will Tuttle will have to marry her now," said one of my companions.

I remember that after such an evening we youngsters walked home rather quietly in the darkness. I boarded at the house of one Trundle, a teamster, and had to go the last three blocks alone. The man spent his days out of doors doing heavy work and except on Saturdays evenings the house was early silent and dark.

Perhaps I romanticize this whole matter. I cannot quite make out. It seems to me now that, as I stumbled forward over uneven sidewalks in the darkness and sat afterward in the darkness on the Trundles' front porch looking at the blue-black summer sky and listening to the occasional night noises, the barking of a dog or the sharp sound of hoof beats on a distant road where some young farmhand was hurrying homeward after an evening in town with his girl; that at such moments something happened to me more deeply significant in my own life than any number of millions of tons of coal mined in a year, the profits and losses of coal mining companies, or the wage to be paid miners. For an hour I sat, and it seems to me that in that hour and by way of the old carpet-bagger something came floating down to me from many men of the old times who, on distant hills and in the streets of cities of an older world, had made songs that now were being resung within me. Sentences that, when the old man read them, had not issued clearly from among the march of many sentences now stepped forth and got themselves looked at and listened to. My lips reformed the sentences the lips of men now dead had formed and, perhaps, caught a little the rhythm, the swing, and the significance of them, and I am sure something of the same sort must have happened to the other lads who had spent the evening with me in the company of the old man. I was at that time intent upon learning the mysteries of the house-painters' trade and as I went through the streets on the next day clad in my overalls I perhaps met one of my companions of the evening before. We stopped and stood talking for a moment. Then he threw his arms above his head and began stretching and yawning. "I didn't get to sleep very early last night. After I went to bed I got to thinking and couldn't sleep at all," he said.

KING COAL. The whole point of which meandering tale being, I think, that it is entirely possible that we Americans may some day awaken to find we have long been traveling a blind trail toward fullness of life. It is true, isn't it, that what we want is leisure, a chance to live more fully? Does not the preamble to our Declaration of Independence say something about the pursuit of happiness?

For my own part the people I know and love all live in industrial towns and are all in some way slaves to that giant we have disturbed in his sleep under the ground, disturbed without really putting the harness upon him. I rather expect I shall myself live and die in such towns and I do not like the prospect, even though I may care greatly for the people who are in the same fix as myself. Things have moved with unbelievable rapidity in not only one but a thousand towns of Mid-America since I sat with my comrades on the porch of the carpet-bagger's house and heard from his lips the voices of poets. Within the year I have re-visited that place.

On the particular street along which we looked on the summer evenings now stands a long row of factories, their grim walls reëchoing at night to the footsteps of a new kind of men. It is quite true and must not be denied. The America of today is not the America of a very few years ago. As to the future America: can a youth spent at the movies, spent whirling through the streets in motor cars, or in the grim residence districts that almost inevitably grow up about factories in our towns or cities, be of the same quality as the youth of the last generation? Surely not. I do not deny to this newer youth its quality. Perhaps the only trouble with me is that there is something here I cannot digest. You see I'm only asking questions after all.

KING COAL.

And there is one question keeps coming back and back, whenever my mind gets on this subject. It seems to me that love has much to do with the fiber and quality of men as citizens of a country and the whole matter of hustling pushing coal-mining factory-building modern life for the most part remains in my mind in the form of annoying and to me unanswerable questions. I find myself going about day after day and asking myself such questions as these: "Can a man love a coal mine or a coal-mining town, a factory, a real-estate boomer, the Twentieth Century Limited, a Ford, a movie or a movie actress, a modern daily newspaper, or a freight car? If a man live in a street in a modern industrial town can he love that street? If a man does not love the little patch of ground on which his own house may stand can he in any sense love the street, the city, the state, the country of which it is a part?" The questions are disquieting. The love of country is to my mind a necessary part of a full and happy life and I do not like to think that love of country may in the end be a thing like modern religion, occasionally pumped into temporary life by some political Billy Sunday and by propaganda in the newspapers.

Well, I write freely when I write what I feel and my own feeling is that coal and the industrial power that has come from coal and the coal mines is now king. The black giant, disturbed in his sleep, has set forth and has conquered. We all breathe his black breath.

Also I believe that self-respecting men, once they have accepted a town or a country as their town or country, do want to bring something like beauty into the place where their lives are to be lived and that in this king there is as yet little beauty. Having been disturbed in his bed in the hills he has set out, Hunlike, to conquer and will conquer. Even as I write he is on the march, with a vanguard of Rotary Club members, invading new towns, building newer and larger cities, breathing his black breath over greater and greater stretches of green country.

The king is, I admit, King.

KING COAL.

What a laugh the word "democracy" must sometimes stir within his black bowels!

. . . . .

May one be ribald when a King is crowned? It has long been my desire to be a little worm in the fair apple of Progress.

As I sit writing and feeling very important and serious about this whole matter of what coal and industrialism is doing to the towns of the Middle West I do have to stop and for a sane moment think that I know little of the matter about which I have made all these words. And it happens I am at this moment sitting in one of the few spots in America where coal is not king.

Perched out on the lip of that Mississippi River that drains nearly the whole of Mid-America there is a city within a city. Where the new and modern city of New Orleans begins, some ten city blocks away from where I sit, the king is King; but in this old French and Creole town, hidden away, half forgotten in its corner, we can make him sing low.

It is afternoon and cool here, and the night will be cooler. I shiver a little as I sit writing of that Coal King who is making so many great fires burn in so many places. I look at my empty fireplace.

From the street there comes a cry that is also a song. I run out on my little balcony and look down. A ragged negro is driving a bony horse along the street and to the horse is hitched a wagon with wobbly wheels. There are a dozen bushels of coal in the wagon and the driver has made himself a song.

"Do you want any coal?
It's gwy'an be cold.
Do you want any coal?
It's gwy'an be cold."

Is he one who sells three buckets of coal for four bits or does he give but two? There is a moment of intense mutual inspection and then from a window on the floor below my landlady comes to my rescue. She speaks sharply a few words of Creole French and a delightful grin spreads over the black face. "Sho, boss. Three heapen ones," he says, and comes up the stairway with my portion of fire and comfort in a broken bushel basket on his shoulder. He is preceded by my friend the landlady who has brought an old iron tub to sit beside my hearth and hold the coal.

And so all is well. I sit and contemplate mankind and such things as social progress or decay with a calm mind.

Why not? My fire burns! The King has been humbled.

The King is in a washtub and I burn his bones.

KING COAL.

Another delightful thought comes. In the end the King may lose the battle, after all. It would be a delicious outcome of the whole affair if, gradually, year after year, an ever and ever increasing number of men should decide that the spoils offered in the King's service were not worth the price of service and should manage in some way to get the King at last into a place where he is compelled to coo him softly like a suckling dove, as he does here in this forgotten spot where Progress is unknown.

# NOTES OUT OF A MAN'S LIFE

## NOTES OUT OF A MAN'S LIFE[1]



### NOTE 23

If some white artist could go among the negroes and live with them much beautiful stuff might be got. The trouble is that no American white man could do it without self-consciousness. The best thing is to stand aside, listen and wait. If I can be impersonal in the presence of black laborers, watch the dance of bodies, hear the song, I may learn something.

### NOTE 24

A dream—I saw a tall fine-looking man with a light coming from his forehead. Everything hung suspended in space. A beautiful, rather sensual-looking woman, quite naked, was half turned, in just the position taken by a baseball pitcher about to throw a ball.

Later, I saw negro women framed by windows as pictures are framed. There were no buildings, just the framed windows floating in space.

[1] New Orleans, 1925.

At each window was a negro woman and they were all old. They were old house servants, field hands, cotton pickers. As I saw each face the woman's whole story was revealed. Years of labor close down to the soil, the soil running through the fingers. When they were young women, nights sitting by a river or by a bayou. Dark earth-floored cabins. The big house of the whites, with lights shining in the distance.

Sometimes the negro men were violent. They took knives and cut each other.

At other times many negroes sat on the ground together and sang.

The connection between the man with the light in his forehead, the naked white woman and the faces of aged negro women was not much. There are no direct connections made in such dreams. One feels sensuality, wonder, interest, quite naturally—is unashamed, does not try to be logical. It may be that thus the negro gets life. As for myself I leave the fact that I have such dreams to the psychoanalysts.

## NOTE 25

A friend of mine was on a boat coming from the South Seas. On the boat was another American, from the South, from the State of Mississippi. As the night was hot and they could not sleep they sat on the deck talking.

The talk turned to negro life in the American South and the Southerner told a tale.

When he was a young man he, the Southerner, went with another young man to hunt. In the late afternoon they came out of a canebrake and up onto a levee facing the Mississippi River.

At that moment a buggy came tearing along the levee top. It was driven by a young white woman of the neighborhood and she was terribly excited. She kept lashing the horse with a buggy whip and when she saw the white men she screamed.

The white men managed to stop the horse and inquired the reason for her terror. A negro man had come alone out of the canebrake a half mile below.

She had been frightened. Many terrible things, she reminded them, had happened in the South.

The young white men ran along the levee, their guns in their hands. When they came to the negro, a man of thirty-five and the father of a family, they presented their guns and made him march before them into the canebrake. They kept swearing, "You black son of a bitch." As they tied him securely to a tree he kept protesting. What had he done? "You know well enough, you black son of a bitch."

When they had him tied one of them took his

hunting knife and cut off an ear. Then he handed the knife to his friend who took the other ear. They were collecting souvenirs of the occasion.

The negro man was left tied in the canebrake several hours. It was very hot and the mosquitoes came in swarms. Later, other negroes came and cut him loose.

The two young men dried the ears and kept them. The man on the boat, when he had told the story, went down to his cabin to get his dried ear and show it. He seemed to think it—my friend said—a symbol of the superiority of the whites.

## NOTE 26

Dreamed of running horses. Their names sang in my head all night. In my dreams, when they were running, they ran to a rhythm produced by the chanting of the names. Something in me seemed to flow with the names, with the bodies of the horses.

## NOTE 27

The Mississippi River drives me to despair. I go to it every day, spend hours walking beside it. I get on boats and travel up and down the river. Stories should be so written that they flow toward their inevitable end as majestically and powerfully as the great river flows down to the Gulf.



NOTE 28

Business men, workers, and others not directly concerned with the arts think of all practicing artists as a race apart. There is no discrimination. All writers, painters, musicians, actors, are put in one class. An Irvin Cobb, a Harold Bell Wright, a Henry Fielding, a Dreiser, a De Foe—it is all one thing.

To know such men at all your occupation must be concealed. When I travel about I become what my fancy at the moment dictates. I am a cotton planter, a fireman from Cleveland, Ohio, taking a vacation, a horse owner, a gambler.

Being a gambler or horse owner goes best. Something about my looks betrays me when I pick out other occupations. In the popular mind the artist is easier associated, perhaps not unfairly, with the gambler, the sport, or the criminal.

NOTE 29

He was a manufacturer's agent in New Orleans and sold printers' ink. The storeroom where he kept his supplies was in the old city, near the Museum and the old Cathedral. It is delightful to walk in that part of the old city, just as evening comes, when the light is uncertain.

I used to see him at work in the dark storehouse under an electric lamp and one evening I went in.

He was making a wooden model of an American clipper ship and it was lovely.

I asked him about it. This is the tale he told me. He was fifty-five. His wife was dead and his children were married. He had never been a great success in business. Once he made considerable money—but later.

He had got an agency—selling printers' ink in New Orleans. In his younger years he lived in a Northern city where men hustled more. In New Orleans he could take things easier. Rents were lower. He knew a good many small printers. They bought ink from him. Why not? He sold good ink. The price was all right.

One day he was in the Museum where there are a good many rather fine models of old ships. New Orleans is a seafaring town. In the old days of sailing ships a good many sailors used to carve such models of ships during long voyages.

In the Museum there was a man from the state university of an interior state. He had come to New Orleans to buy models of old ships but there were none to be found. Nowadays they are picked up by curio dealers who buy them at a high price. The rich want them to put on library shelves above the books. They are no doubt made now in some factory.

The man from the interior was puzzled. Could a man be found who would carve from models in the museum a few such ships?

The wholesale dealer in ink stepped forward. "I'll do it," he said. He had never carved anything but when he was a boy in Philadelphia he spent a great deal of time in the shipping. At night, as a boy, he dreamed of ships.

The man seeking ship models asked him how much he would charge. "Thirty dollars each. It will take me a long time. I won't ask you to pay me anything down. When I have completed the models, if you do not like them, it will be all right."

The whole affair, the old man told me, had been foolish enough. He had never used tools. Books concerning ships had to be bought. His hands had to be trained.

When I saw him he was completing the first model that satisfied him. It was the fourth one he had attempted and the first three had been burned.

"Will you do the others?" I asked. "Surely," he said. He worked every evening from six

NOTES OUT OF A MAN'S LIFE.

until nearly midnight. He had never been so well, so contented. "The whole foolish business has cost me nearly two hundred dollars. It is the only thing I ever did that gave me any real satisfaction," he said.

THE END